BEYOND IRAQ: THE NEXT MOVE

Ancient Prophecy and Modern Conspiracy Collide

Michael D. Evans

WS

WHITE STONE BOOKS

LAKELAND, FLORIDA

07 06 05 04 03   10 9 8 7 6 5 4 3 2 1

Beyond Iraq: The Next Move
Ancient Prophecy and Modern Conspiracy Collide
ISBN 1-59379-010-4
Copyright © 2003 by Michael D. Evans

Published by White Stone Books, Inc.
P.O. Box 2835
Lakeland, Florida 33806

Dedication

This book is dedicated to the great men and women who do not seek the praises of men, but who desire to remain in the shadows... the glue that holds great nations together..."A" players in the chess game of life who chose to remain in "C" roles...those who will not compromise moral principles and biblical values, and are determined to light a candle rather than curse the darkness... believing that prayer is not the last resort, but the first, and most important resort.

Acknowledgments

Special thanks to my publisher, whose faith in me and this book, and whose amazing gifts, made it all happen. To all the team at White Stone Books who were a tremendous support. To my beloved wife, Carolyn, who endured my 20-hour writing days, and who pulled all-nighters with me. To my executive assistant, Lanelle Young, who stayed calm under pressure, and was a fantastic help. To Ilan Chaim who tolerated my need-it-now emails throughout the writing of this book, and to my dear friends in Israel whose wisdom has been an enormous help. They number in the hundreds...from generals to intelligence experts to former prime ministers. I especially want to thank two old friends from whom I have drawn strength and inspiration over the last 25 years, Vice Premier Ehud Olmert (Government of Israel), and Binyamin Netanyahu, former prime minister, and presently Minister of Finance. And, to the Jerusalem Prayer Team, whose prayer, faith, and support for this project has been absolutely tremendous.

Contents

The CIA
Original Headquarters Building,
Main Lobby

etched into the wall
to characterize the intelligence mission of a free society.

"And ye shall know the Truth and the Truth shall set you free."
John VIII-XXXII

Preface

I looked deeply into the intense smiling eyes of Rudolph Giuliani. As I sat in his office contemplating the next question of my interview, my eyes fell on a picture over his right shoulder of three firemen holding up an American flag atop the rubble of what was once the World Trade Center. "This is my last question," I said. Then I asked it.

To be quite honest, I don't even remember what it was, because as New York's most famous mayor leaned forward and began to speak, I suddenly saw in his eyes a small thin man holding out a tray of cookies and tea. I recognized him as Isser Harel, the founder of the Mossad (Israel's intelligence agency). I was sitting in his home, and it was a memory from roughly 23 years earlier.

"Will terrorism come to America?" Harel repeated my question back to me. "America has the power to fight terrorism, but not the will; the terrorists have the will, but not the power. But all of that could change in time. Oil buys more than tents. You in the West kill a fly and rejoice. In the Middle East, we kill one, and one hundred flies come to the funeral."

"Yes, I fear it will come in time."

"Where will it come?" I asked him.

He thought for a moment. "New York is the symbol of your freedom and capitalism. It's likely they will strike there first at your tallest building, which is a symbol of your power."

Suddenly I remembered the exact date of the conversation. It had taken place on September 23, 1980.[1] "Thanks, Mike," Mr. Giuliani said, then he stood, extending a kind, warm hand towards mine.

I had completely missed his answer! I would have died of embarrassment if he had known that I was having a flashback — more like a nightmare — right in the middle of his response.

As I stood and shook Mayor Giuliani's hand, all I could see in my mind's eye were the two 189-ton bombs in the form of fully fueled Boeing 767s hitting the World Trade Towers just as my friend had foretold. No one could have possibly known that on that Tuesday, the 11th of September, 2001, the first war of the 21st century would begin — a war against terror that may well draw the line in the sand, forever dividing light from darkness, proclaiming like a trumpet a spiritual battle of monumental proportions. Who would have wondered at the time, that the epicenters of this battle would center on ancient Babylon (biblical Iraq)—the spiritual center of darkness—and Jerusalem—the spiritual center of Light.

Our meeting was on Thursday, March 13, 2003. Little did I know that in six days' time America would be taking the war against terrorism to Iraq and an American September 11th flag from New York would soon be hanging on the head of Saddam's image in Baghdad.

As President George W. Bush had said in addressing a joint session of Congress and the American people on September 20, 2001, "Our enemy is a radical network of terrorists, and every government that supports them. Our war on terror begins with Al-Qaida, but it does not end there. It will not end until every terrorist group of global reach has been found, stopped, and defeated…. Either you are with us, or you are with the terrorists. From this day forward, any nation that continues to harbor or support terrorism will be regarded by the United States as a hostile regime."[2] His message, in essence, was clear: The U.S. will take this war to any country who participates in, gives aid to, or harbors terrorists. He drew the line in the sands of the Arabian Peninsula—there is no more room for covert support of terrorism: *Either you are with us, or you are with the terrorists.* (I believe that.) Iraq will become the U.S. base from which the war on terrorism in the Middle East is fought. From there it will only be a short reach to the throat of Syria and Iran and the terrorist networks.

As it turns out, Iraq, the remnant of ancient Babylon and a known supporter of terrorist organizations, was the first country to openly defy the United States' warning to disarm or be disarmed. Roughly a month before this writing, the U.S.-led Coalition invaded Iraq against the wishes of many of its allies with the purpose of stopping terrorists before they strike again with the more deadly forces of chemical, biological, or nuclear weapons. It is a struggle between good and evil, but I believe it is even more profound than that: It may well be the setting up of a chessboard dividing the players for an apocalyptic battle prophesied in Daniel, Jeremiah, and Revelation.

As I was finishing the chapter in this book on how the road map from Baghdad leads to Jerusalem and what the prophetic implications of that could be, I reviewed my notes on the man that the Quartet (Russia, the E.U., the U.N., and the U.S.) had approved as the Palestinian Authority's new Prime Minister: Mahmoud Abbas (also known as Abu Mazen). He was Arafat's longtime Deputy—a shady character at best. He believes that the Holocaust was a myth and stated, "The *intifada* [the Palestinian uprising against Israel] must continue…. It is the right of the Palestine people to resist and use all possible means in order to defend its presence and existence," in a March 3, 2003, interview in the *Alsharak Alawast* newspaper. (This was a blanket endorsement of terrorists' acts and suicide bombings.) Abbas was also among those who pressed Arafat to reject Israel's comprehensive peace proposal at Camp David in 2000, which offered them 95 percent of the land that was captured in the 1967 Six Day War. "Palestinians should have no regrets about refusing Israel's offer of 95 percent of the land," Abbas later said, "because 95 percent is not 100 percent." Abbas is among those who insist that Israel surrender every centimeter of the land Israel took in 1967 in self-defense from Jordan, which includes the Old City of Jerusalem and its holy Jewish and Christian sites. He also wants unlimited immigration rights for Palestinians into the new, smaller Jewish state established after this. Those two acts would, of course, spell out the end of the nation of Israel.

Turning briefly from my notes to collect my thoughts, I noticed the face of Secretary of State Colin Powell on a small TV I normally leave on to C-Span to catch the latest from Washington, D.C. I suddenly jerked forward and turned it up a little so that I could hear him better. Little did I know that like two prophets, each would touch the nerve centers of prophecy—darkness and light—Babylon and Jerusalem. (By the way, this was on March 30, 2003—Day 12 of Operation Iraqi Freedom.) Colin Powell stood to his feet and looked into the eyes of Israeli Foreign Minister Silvan Shalom:

"I am very pleased to be sharing this stage with my new colleague, Minister Silvan Shalom….
"War and force were not our first choices. We gave diplomacy a chance."

He continued on:

"Syria also now faces a critical choice. Syria can continue direct support for terrorist groups and the dying regime of Saddam Hussein, or it can embark on a different and more hopeful course. Either way, Syria bears the responsibility for its choices, and for the consequences."

Again he continued:

"Once the new Prime Minister is confirmed in office [referring to Abbas, who had not yet been confirmed as Palestinian Prime Minister by the Palestinian Legislative Council], we will present both sides with the Road Map we have developed to restart the movement toward peace…. The Road Map—that we have developed in close consultation with the parties: our friends in the region and our partners in the Quartet—describes that journey and the mutual obligation both sides must meet if we are to reach our shared destination."[3]

I looked on in shock. *What shared destination? Not Israel's! They would have to be dragged kicking and screaming to sign like in 1991 when they were forced to sign the Middle East Peace Agreement in Madrid,* I thought.

Foreign Minister Silvan Shalom then stood and began to speak:[4]

"It is a special honor to greet Secretary of State Colin Powell, who just delivered an inspiring speech. Members of Congress and the diplomatic corps,…even as we speak, allied forces are engaged in combat in Iraq…. Operation Iraqi Freedom is advancing. It is not a simple undertaking and involves high risk….
"The tyranny of Iraqi rulers today has its roots in the ancient Babylon of biblical times. The prophet Jeremiah referred to the dangers posed by Babylon, Iraq of today, to the region and to God's punishment for the cruel despots of the land of two rivers. Some would say Jeremiah prophesied current events. He said, and I quote, 'I will raise against Babylon an assembly of great nations from the north country, for she has sinned against God.'"[5]

Only five days after these speeches by Secretary of State Powell and Foreign Minister Shalom, and before Abbas was confirmed, I heard my fax machine printing a document entitled "UNCLASSIFIED." It began:

"The following is an unofficial translation of the U.S. 'Road Map' plan, which the Palestinian National Authority received the day before yesterday officially and in writing from the U.S. Administration...."[6]

As I read through the Road Map I noticed the last words on page 10:

"AMEMBASSY CAIRO (American Embassy Cairo)
UNMISSION GENEVA (U.N. Mission Geneva)
AMCOUNSUL JEDDAH (American Consulate Jeddah)
AMCONSUL JERUSALEM (American Consulate Jerusalem)
AMEMBASSY NICOSIA (American Embassy Nicosia)
AMEMBASSY TUNIS (American Embassy Tunis)
AMEMBASSY VIENNA (American Embassy Vienna)"

Then a few days later, on Tuesday, April 8, 2003, and still before Abbas was confirmed, President Bush and Prime Minister Tony Blair spoke at the conclusion of their third Operation Freedom Summit in Hillsborough, Northern Ireland. At this time President Bush—whom I personally admire—said this of Abbas: "I'm pleased with the new leader of the Palestinian Authority. I look forward to him finally putting his cabinet in place so we can release the Road Map."

In its quest to liberate Iraq, America launched a war of biblical proportions—all the while with a plan to force tiny Israel, our most trusted ally in the region, to pay the bill of appeasement with land once more tucked quietly and confidently away in the liberal U.S. State Department's back pocket.

Who are the players behind this collision between ancient prophecy and modern conspiracy?

What is the Road Map and why is it a threat to the lives of all Americans?

Is America's war with Iraq in biblical prophecy?

Could George W. Bush be making prophetic mistakes by listening to liberals' advice?

Could this be the beginning of the struggle that will set the stage for Armageddon?

If we look closely at the evidence, the answer to most of these questions may very well be a resounding, "Yes."

Michael D. Evans
Good Friday/Passover
April 18, 2003

Israel Today

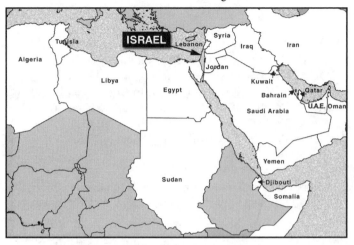

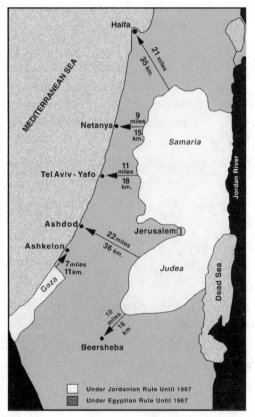

Israel, if Road Map is implemented

1

ANSWERING THE WAKE-UP CALL FROM HELL

"September 11th was a wake-up call from hell that has opened our eyes to the horrors that await us tomorrow if we fail to act today."

Binyamin Netanyahu
Then Prime Minister of Israel, speaking before the
U.S. House of Representatives Government Reform Committee
on September 20th, 2001

No one could ever have predicted that the beginning of the 21st century would find the United States at war with an enemy with no borders, no conventional military, and no specific nationality—an enemy with literally no face. This new warfare, though, has proven to be the ultimate chess match with thousands of pawns and all of the kings and queens hidden from view. The pawns are sent forth to die and take as many people with them as they can, while the world watches wondering where, how, and when they will strike next. Ironically the Quartet has chosen to make Israel into the Political Pawn in the midst of the game. Suicide bombers taking out dozens was horrible and ghastly on the buses and in the restaurants of Tel Aviv or Jerusalem, but the U.S. could still look away. September 11, 2001, changed that—turning fiction into fact, and the unimaginable into the real. That single day of horror alerted most Americans to the grave dangers that are now facing our world.

Today terrorists have access to chemical and biological weapons that can kill tens of thousands in a matter of minutes. Extremist Islamic terrorist organizations nullify the need to have air power or intercontinental missiles as delivery systems for an Islamic nuclear payload. The terrorists themselves will be the delivery system. In the worst of such scenarios, the consequences would be not a car bomb, but a nuclear bomb. With the new threat of thousands—if not millions—dying at a time in the case of terrorists employing chemical, biological, or nuclear weapons, the only logical alternative has been to seek out the terrorists before they strike and eliminate the governments or powers that enable them. Many would think that Iraq was just the first on this list, but when you look at both history and scripture, the battle for Baghdad takes on much more profound and prophetic tones.

Why Was the War on Terrorism Taken to Baghdad?

Osama bin Laden, who is believed to have been the "godfather" behind the September 11th attacks, issued a statement called the "Nuclear Bomb of Islam." In it he said, "The international Islamic front for fighting the Jews and Crusaders is the duty of all Muslims." He called on all Muslims to "prepare for as much force as possible to terrorize the enemies of Allah."[1]

Terrorism is now a direct confrontation against "The Great Satan—America," who in the eyes of the bin Ladens of the world is desecrating the cradle of Islam. Bin Laden's terrorist network Al-Qaida ("The Base") is a coalition of the most diabolical terrorist organizations in the world, all linked together with a common cause—to attack what they believe to be the kingdoms of evil— the great Satan, America, and the little Satan, Israel. The actions of bin Laden and his terrorist links could not be possible without a broad infrastructure of government movements and organizations that support terror directly or indirectly.

Today is April 13th, 2003, day 26 of the war, as America advances painfully, but victoriously, in Operation Iraqi Freedom. The relentless search for the "10-billion-dollar man,"[2] Saddam Hussein, continues along with the search for weapons of mass destruction. U.S. National Security Advisor Condoleezza Rice is meeting today with Dov Weisglass, chief of staff for the Prime Minister of Israel. Israel is urgently appealing to the U.S. to make changes in the Road Map.

President Bush said on April 12th, "Chemicals of mass destruction are in Syria."[3] On that same day, the White House also demanded Syria stop harboring Saddam's government officials, and said that Huda Salih Mahdi Ammash, and Rihad Taha ("Chemical Sally" and "Dr. Germ") from Baghdad were in Damascus.[4] French Foreign Minister Dominique de Villepin said on the same day in Cairo, Egypt: "The U.S. needs to stop putting pressure on Syria and start putting pressure on Israel." De Villepin said it is time for the "Road Map," and that France was "prepared to host a peace conference."[5]

And, the search for Osama bin Laden continues. With the release of an audiotape from bin Laden on February 11, 2003,[6] it appears that the ringleader of Al-Qaida terrorist network is still very much alive and as great a threat as ever. He openly linked arms with

> *Capturing bin Laden and dethroning Hussein will not be enough.*

Saddam Hussein as he admonished the Iraqi people to rise up against the "American infidels." But capturing bin Laden and dethroning Hussein will not be enough. Like a team sport, terrorism is a team effort. To combat it, America must focus on the whole team of opponents instead of just individual players.

Even in World War II, America was not forced to confront suicide bombers on its own soil. We never concluded, in WWII, we could win the war by shooting down one suicide bomber. The victory obviously required more systemic measures. Likewise, to truly defeat terrorism, we need to open our eyes to the obvious — that Osama bin Laden is a card-carrying member of a terrorist cartel who is received with honor by the Saddam Husseins of the Middle East (the terrorist states) — and then direct bold efforts to stop him and aggressively stifle the entire scope and network of terrorist activity.

Terrorism shows itself to us today with a 21st century makeover. Today, terrorist states generally don't take hostages.

Incognito—invisible—they can pose greater psychological damage by paralyzing, confusing, and diminishing the ability of a nation to retaliate. Young terrorists are used as Jihad bait by elusive terrorist states and organizations. It's a "don't ask, don't tell" world where the sponsors, with tears in their eyes, innocently express their condolences to victimized countries.

Organized crime is about greed. Terrorism is about glory—the glory of humiliating "The Great Satan—America," the glory of believing that all of the terrorists' family members are guaranteed a place in Heaven because of their acts, and that, as young men, they will be greeted in Heaven with a room full of voluptuous virgins.

> *Organized crime is about greed. Terrorism is about glory.*

Does it seem a little strange that Syria, Iran, Libya, or even the P.L.O. have never turned a terrorist who has killed Americans over to America? Not even the terrorist who killed Leon Klinghoffer who was on the cruise ship the *Achille Lauro*[7]—a defenseless old man in a wheelchair whose body and chair they threw overboard after they killed him. Leon Klinghoffer and his wife, Marilyn, took the cruise to celebrate their 36th wedding anniversary. Is this the reason for the dancing in the streets? It's the theater of the absurd, and a festival of hypocrisy!

Abu Abbas was a member of the Palestine Liberation Organization's executive committee from 1984 to 1991, according to the U.S. State Department. The U.S. Justice Department has said it has no grounds to seek his extradition as there are no outstanding warrants against him. Abbas was captured by the U.S. Special Operations Forces during a series of raids around Baghdad on Monday, April 16, 2003. He is going to be a major test for the Bush Doctrine on the war on terrorism. Will there now be "good terrorists" and "bad terrorists"? According to Reuters [April 16, 2003], The Palestine Authority demanded the release of veteran Palestinian guerrilla leader Abu Abbas on Wednesday.

The PA spokesperson said that the detention of Abbas in Iraq by U.S. forces violated an interim Middle East peace deal:

"We demand the United States release Abu Abbas. It has no right to imprison him," Palestinian cabinet minister Saeb Erekat told Reuters. "The Palestinian-Israeli interim agreement signed on September 28, 1995, stated that members of the Palestinian Liberation Organization must not be detained or tried for matters they committed before the Oslo Peace Accord of September 13, 1993," Erekat said. He added, "This interim agreement was signed on the U.S. side by President Clinton and his Secretary of State, Warren Christopher.

The terrorist crosshairs are on America, a nation they see as the pig polluting the world with her prosperity, power, and pornography, infecting the Islamic vision with her moral and religious perversion. Yet while terrorism hides behind the veil of jihad—holy war upon an immoral enemy—the real issue is not truth, but greed and jealousy. The terrorists hate America because it is blessed, and they are not.

When I asked a Saudi General during the Gulf War, "Why are the United States and Israel so hated by Muslims?" he responded with a smile, "Oh, no, take heart. They don't *all* hate you. Only the extremely religious fundamentalists hate you and that may not be more than 5 to 10 percent of the Muslim world—only 50 to 100 million people.

"But why do they hate you, Mike? Because your country is so powerful, and Israel is so powerful even though they are a small country. Do you know how humiliating that is to have to acknowledge that the 'crusaders'—America and Zionist Israel—have more power than we do? We carry the vision of Islam in our bosoms—a vision of world domination where Islam will cover the entire world because of its power."

Sheikh Omar Abdel Rahman, spiritual leader of the World Trade Center bombers in 1993, said, "The obligation of Allah is upon us to wage Jihad for the sake of Allah.... We have to thoroughly demoralize the enemies of Allah by blowing up their towers that constitute the pillars of their civilization…the high buildings of which they are so proud."[8] They didn't attack the Playboy mansion or a beer distillery; they struck at the symbols of our prosperity.

The New York police found 47 boxes of Rahman's terrorist literature. The F.B.I. wrote on the boxes, "Irrelevant religious stuff."[9] Rahman, who was involved in the assassination of Egyptian President Anwar Sadat, came to America in 1990, free to set up his terrorist shop in New Jersey as if with our blessing.

PBS, in a piece aired in 1994,[10] described the terrorist team effort. The documentary revealed the threat of a quilt-work of Islamic groups and terrorist sponsors that have sprung up across America since the Iranian revolution. These groups include arms of Islamic Jihad, Hamas, and Hizbullah with cells in New York, Florida, Chicago, Kansas City, and Dallas. The groups hide behind a smoke screen of small businesses and religious and charitable Islamic groups. These team members work in the U.S. to raise funds, recruit volunteers, and lay plans for terrorist missions for the ultimate battle against "The Great Satan." Their primary objective is to succeed in the mission without being blamed, then to realize widespread media coverage, and to maximize psychological and economic damage through terror.

On September 11th, *Al-Ayyam*, Arafat's P.L.O.-controlled newspaper said, "The suicide bombers of today are the noble successors of the Lebanese suicide bombers who taught U.S. Marines a tough lesson. These suicide bombers are the salt of the earth, the engine of history. They are the most noble people among us."

America is focusing on the terrorist cartel and working aggressively with other nations to cut it off—like the head of a poisonous snake. As long as we allow organizations to harbor terrorists, and countries to empower them and reward them, the network will thrive. Confronting Iraq is only the first step in this process, but it is also a sign to the other nations supporting terrorism that we are serious. If we want the terrorists to fear us—and that is the only thing they respect—then we must remove the ideology of good terrorist and bad terrorist from our vocabulary. All terrorists are bad and no terrorist must be given the time of day. Countries and organizations that harbor terrorists should not even be able to spit in the wind without it coming back in their faces.

If America maintains its resolve to deal aggressively with terrorists through economic and military retaliation, the family of terrorism will fragment, and no longer will terrorism be a coordinated team effort. But if we don't stand boldly against all terrorism, the power brokers of the world will force our nation to redefine the meaning of terrorism.

As if good terrorist organizations must be rewarded and bad ones punished! We will be sending a signal to millions of raging Islamic fundamentalists that we fear them and they will come upon us like a plague. No, not with big bombs, but little ones—bombs strapped to the backs of suicide bombers—the most dangerous weapon on the planet, which cannot be defended against either in Iraq or America! This weapon of choice works best when things are calm. Prayer is needed now more than ever. It has been said that the only thing needed for evil to prevail is for good people to do nothing.

Iraq Will Not Be the End

President George W. Bush declared after September 11th, "We will take the war to the terrorists."[11]That is precisely what we are now doing. Baghdad is the new ground zero, joined at the hip to regimes on its border that harbor, aid, and abet terror. America must win the war on terrorism and in order to do that we must route out the approximately two-dozen terrorist organizations that make up the cartel of Islamic fundamentalism. The key to defeating terrorism lies in terrorist-harboring states that aid and abet terror.

Yet as strong as we are in the natural, this is a spiritual battle. As Paul said:

Finally, my brethren, be strong in the Lord and in the power of His might. Put on the whole armor of God, that you may be able to stand against the wiles of the devil. For we do not wrestle against flesh and blood, but against principalities, against powers, against the rulers of the darkness of this age, against spiritual hosts of wickedness in the heavenly places.

Ephesians 6:10-12

Unless God-fearing Americans fall on their knees and pray, our victory in Iraq will only have addressed the surface issues of political and financial support from one regime. Unless we are willing to pray and take on the demons behind terrorism, the faceless enemy will just move house to strike from somewhere else. We routed the political power of Hitler, but the spirit that drove his hatred and genocide has just moved on to instigate the terrorism we are experiencing today: bigotry and anti-Semitism; hatred for Christians and Jews. Only moral fortitude and prayer can diffuse the time bomb of hatred that caused both the Holocaust and the attacks of September 11th. Yet if these two spiritual weapons remain safely under lock and key, unused, our children's children may have to fight a battle for the survival of the planet.

For his part, President George W. Bush has been forthright, systematic, and open in the U.S.'s pursuit to disarm terrorism. From his speech of September 20, 2001, to the recognition of Iraq as a member of "the axis of evil" to restarting the U.N. weapons inspectors' efforts to building a coalition to disarm Iraq and depose Hussein, he has shown the determination and the will to follow this course to its end and the world has had no reason to be surprised by our actions. While the face of terrorism has been disguised, the face of its opposition is clearly recognizable.

In a televised speech on March 17, 2003, 8:00 P.M. EST, following numerous warnings to Saddam Hussein to comply with his 1991 pledge to totally disarm and end his 12-year defiance of that condition for ending the Gulf War, President Bush delivered an ultimatum. He stated: "Saddam Hussein and his sons must leave Iraq within 48 hours. Their refusal to do so will result in military conflict commenced at a time of our choosing."

In defying this final ultimatum, Saddam Hussein positioned his regime in Iraq as a target in the war on terrorism. America won the battle for Baghdad. But what events will follow it? In the natural this appears to be the first major step in disarming world terrorism, but the rest of the world has not maintained America's composure and resolve in confronting this threat. While so many stood with us in September of 2001, few were willing to cross the borders with us to confront the enemy. Deposing Hussein will not end terrorism, only hamper it, and ultimately America and Great Britain cannot defeat it alone. Other nations are sitting on the fence and waiting to see what happens next, but that fence is being dismantled. Pretty soon they will have to choose a side. America's hope lies in those who will not compromise moral principles and biblical values and will commit themselves to the power of prayer!

The Coalition forces have cut a smooth and clear line in the Iraqi sand on their way to Baghdad, but when the dust settles, the nations of the world will need to decide which side of that line they are on. In the natural, it is war and politics, but nothing that affects the Bible lands is ever really that simple. In order for the plant of terrorism to be killed, its roots must be dug up and exposed. Any attempt by America to root out global terrorism without plowing under the soil in which it grows, will only spread the virus more quickly, and will guarantee a prescription for failure.

As Bible-believing Americans we must realize that this is a battle between politics and prophecy. We must not sleep in a time of war. The battle is raging and we must pay the price. It's up to us now to take the high ground—and stand up and speak up and pray up!

This is a battle between politics and prophecy.

By faith these people overthrew kingdoms, ruled with justice, and received what God had promised them. They shut the mouths of lions, quenched the flames of fire, and escaped death by the edge of the sword. Their weakness was turned to strength. They became strong in battle and put whole armies to flight.

Hebrews 11:33-34 NLT

This book is a spiritual call to arms, because the real battles are spiritual ones and won through prayer. Only those who will not compromise moral principles and biblical values and will value prayer more than pleasure will be able to truly win this war!

According to the book of Revelation, there are forces beneath Iraq—the area referred to as Babylon or Babylonia in Scripture—that have other targets besides America. Was Silvan Shalom[12] correct in identifying the battle for Baghdad as God mustering the "great nations of the north" for the final assault on Babylon and all the evil it represents?

If so, there is much more at stake here than just the end of terrorism—and if so, that line in the desert will not just divide the sides of this battle, but may determine which side nations will be on for the final battle of the ages.

"You gain strength, courage, and confidence by every experience in which you stop to look fear in the face. You must do that which you think you cannot do."

Eleanor Roosevelt

God is our refuge and strength,
A very present help in trouble.

Therefore we will not fear,
Even though the earth be removed,
And though the mountains be carried into the midst of the sea;

Though its waters roar and be troubled,
Though the mountains shake with its swelling.

Psalm 46:1-3

2

A WAR OF BIBLICAL PROPORTIONS

---

*And another angel followed, saying, "Babylon is fallen, is fallen, that great city, **because she has made all nations drink of the wine of the wrath of her fornication."***

Revelation 14:8 [emphasis in bold added]

The Bible has much to say about the land known today as Iraq. It is said that the Garden of Eden was located there, meaning it was the place where Adam and Eve committed the first sin. The occult and astrology began there. It was to Nineveh, the capital of Mesopotamia and now part of Iraq, that the prophet Jonah was sent by God to call the populace to repent. Scholars believe the city Ur of the Chaldeans was located within Iraq's borders. It was from that city that God called Abraham to go to the land of Canaan. (See Genesis 11:28-12:5.)

Who would ever have imagined that the front page of *The New York Times*, Wednesday, April 16, 2003, would say the following: Iraqi exile leaders, tribal sheiks, ethnic Kurds, and Shiite clerics gathered in a tent near the birthplace of Abraham today and said they would work to create a fully democratic government in Iraq.

Meeting under heavy security at Tallil Air Base here in the presence of American, British, and Polish diplomats, the Iraqis called for an end to the violence and looting that have ravaged the country since the collapse of President Saddam Hussein's government. They issued a statement that included 13 points outlining how they would seek to establish a "federal system" under leaders chosen by the Iraqi people and not "imposed from outside."

The most common biblical name for this region, however, is Babylon (the capital city) or Babylonia (the nation). It was King

Nebuchadnezzar of Babylon who conquered Israel and Judea in 586 B.C., taking captive the Jewish people and imprisoning them in Babylonia for seventy years. It was in Babylon that wicked Nebuchadnezzar threw Shadrach, Meshach, and Abednego into the fiery furnace and King Darius threw Daniel into the lions' den. (See 2 Kings 24; Daniel 2:49; 3:12-30; 6.) And it was from Babylonia that Israel was delivered when Daniel prayed. (See Daniel 9-10.)

It is important to see the first and last mentions of this land in Scripture, though, to understand its significance. The first mention of the area of Iraq is in Genesis 10 and 11 as it was in Iraq that the Tower of Babel was built. The name "Babel" in fact is the Hebrew rendering of the Akkadian "Babylon" which means "the gate of the god." Most scholars place the city of Babylon about 40 miles south of Baghdad. It was the first city man built after the flood. (See Genesis 10:10.) It is referred to 300 times in the Bible and it is the second most mentioned city in the Bible, the first being Jerusalem. It was here that humankind first tried to reach Heaven without God's help, thus setting themselves up as gods and creating the first man-made religion. In the book of Revelation, Babylon is the seat of the Antichrist, the Beast, and the symbol of humankind's adultery in turning away from God to other gods.

In Scripture, Babylon is the seat of Satan's evil as much as Jerusalem is the seat of God's righteousness. In fact, it appears that the sides of the final battle are symbolized by these two cities.

Iraq in Prophecy

While ancient Iraq clearly plays a role in the biblical narrative, it also serves an important purpose in biblical prophecy. Ezekiel's prophecy of the dry bones coming to life (which represents the restoration of Israel) and the one that predicts Armageddon were made in Babylonian Iraq. (See Ezekiel 37-38.)

Because of his opposition to the Jews, Saddam's palace at Babylon and entire "kingdom" will ultimately face destruction as prophesied by Isaiah:

The burden against Babylon which Isaiah the son of Amoz saw....
"Wail, for the day of the LORD is at hand!
It will come as destruction from the Almighty....
"And Babylon, the glory of kingdoms,
The beauty of the Chaldeans' pride,
Will be as when God overthrew Sodom and Gomorrah."

Isaiah 13:1,6,19

He also relayed the final outcome for the man who would be a modern Nebuchadnezzar and threaten all of creation with his terrible weapons:

"I will rise up against them,"
declares the LORD Almighty.
"I will cut off from Babylon her name and survivors,
her offspring and descendants,"
declares the LORD.
"I will turn her into a place for owls
and into swampland;
I will sweep her with the broom of destruction,"
declares the LORD Almighty.

Isaiah 14:22-23 NIV

Daniel's Prophecies

Iraq is the subject of several prophecies in the Book of Daniel as well. King Nebuchadnezzar had dreams of future events, and Daniel interpreted these dreams to explain the vision of a future Babylonian empire. *"There is a God in Heaven who reveals secrets, and He has made known to King Nebuchadnezzar what will be in the latter days* [the end times]" (Daniel 2:28, author's insertion).

First was Daniel's prophetic response to the king of Babylon's amazing dream of a "large statue" (v. 31 NIV.) The setting was Babylon (now Iraq), and the dream was about a battle over the Middle East and ultimately Jerusalem. Daniel revealed that all the nations of the world would be unified and form a "new world order" led by a false Messiah. Although he would deceive the world with a false peace, in the end the King of Kings would defeat him! (v. 34.)

"And in the days of these kings the God of Heaven will set up a kingdom which shall never be destroyed; and the kingdom shall not be left to other people; it shall break in pieces and consume all these kingdoms, and it shall stand forever."

Daniel 2:44

Daniel revealed that a stone would crush all the kingdoms at the end of the age. Likewise, Jesus spoke of the end times in which we are indeed living: *"'The stone which the builders rejected Has become the chief cornerstone.' Whoever falls on that stone will be broken; but on whomever it falls, it will grind him to powder"* (Luke 20:17-18).

Is the world rushing like a whirlwind toward this amazing prophecy? *"Now when these things begin to happen, look up and lift up your heads, because your redemption draws near"* (Luke 21:28).

Daniel's Seventy Weeks

During a time of prayer, the angel Gabriel appeared to Daniel and revealed a timetable of coming events that would especially affect Israel. (See Daniel 9:24-26.) Daniel's vision of seventy weeks is considered to be the backbone of end-time prophecy, giving us a mathematical revelation to recognize the conditions that will occur to indicate that the coming of the Messiah is near. It also foretold His death, the destruction of Jerusalem, the rise of the Antichrist, and the establishment of the Messiah's coming kingdom on earth.

In Daniel 9:27, the prophet revealed that the specific marker that will begin the final seven-year period of the seventy weeks is the making of a covenant of peace between Israel and an immensely powerful leader. The Bible identifies that leader as the Antichrist. He will offer solutions to the perplexing problems and international crises that threaten the very existence of the world.

At first everything will appear to be going well. The centuries of armed tension will be relieved. By the peace imposed through the power of the Antichrist, Israel will be able to turn its full attention to the development of the country and its resources and will prosper as never before. The rebuilding of the Temple in Jerusalem and the resumption of sacrifices and oblations will even be permitted.

But just when peace seems to have come for Israel, it will be taken from her. After three and one-half years, the Antichrist will break his treaty with Israel. He will go to the Temple and cause the sacrifices and offerings to cease and bring about the "abomination of desolation" by proclaiming himself to be God. (See Daniel 11:31.)

Best-selling author, Dr. Tim LaHaye, asked me while filming for his movie *Armageddon*, "Mike, how do you think the Jews in Israel will respond to *Armageddon?*"

I said, "The same way the rest of the world will—with terror."

Yes, I truly believe that America's war with Iraq was indeed prophesied in the Bible by the prophet Jeremiah:

> *For behold, I will raise and cause to come up against Babylon*
> *An assembly of great nations from the north country,*
> *And they shall array themselves against her;*
> *From there she shall be captured.*
> *Their arrows shall be like those of an expert warrior;*
> *None shall return in vain.*

Jeremiah 50:9

There is no way Jeremiah could have been able to understand what the U.S. was going to do with laser guided bombs that indeed were "expert arrows" that did not return in vain.

Again, another of Jeremiah's amazing prophecies in the 51st chapter is quite astonishing; the world sees the images of Saddam falling all over the Baghdad, but they never read this:

> *"Therefore behold, the days are coming*
> *That I will bring judgment on the carved images of Babylon;*

Her whole land shall be ashamed,
And all her slain shall fall in her midst.
Then the Heavens and the earth and all that is in them
Shall sing joyously over Babylon;
For the plunderers shall come to her from the north, *says the LORD.*
Jeremiah 51:47-48 [emphasis in bold added]

Isaiah the prophet also described an amazing sight:

For thus has the Lord said to me:
"Go, set a watchman,
Let him declare what he sees."
And he saw a chariot with a pair of horsemen,
A chariot of donkeys, and a chariot of camels,
And he listened earnestly with great care.
Then he cried, "A lion, my Lord!
I stand continually on the watchtower in the daytime;
I have sat at my post every night.
*And look, here comes a chariot of men **with** a pair of horsemen!"*
Then he answered and said,
"Babylon is fallen, is fallen!
And all the carved images of her gods
He has broken to the ground."
Isaiah 21:6-9

He says it's a "lion" and goes on tell about a "chariot of men with horses"—perhaps an Abrams tank! He goes on to say, *"Babylon...is fallen! And all the carved images of her gods He has broken to the ground."* Who will ever forget seeing the fall of Baghdad and the image of Saddam—who considered himself a god—falling over and the head breaking off as an Abrams tank pulled it down? And then the Iraqis pulling the head through the street? Nor the plundering of *Al-Qurna* (the Garden of Eden) that has turned it into a wasteland.

Nor will anyone forget the tragic plundering by a lawless society of 170,000 ancient and priceless artifacts on Friday, April 11, 2003, at the Iraqi National Museum in Baghdad. The artifacts covered the entire 7,000-year history or Babylon.

Iraq Prophesied in the New Testament?

Does the New Testament also predict the destruction of Iraq? When John the Revelator was on the Isle of Patmos, God revealed the answer of this mystery to him. He heard the following:

> *"Babylon the great is fallen, is fallen, and has become a dwelling place of demons, a prison for every foul spirit, and a cage for every unclean and hated bird!...*
> *"Therefore her plagues will come in one day—death and mourning and famine. And she will be utterly burned with fire....*
> *"Thus with violence the great city Babylon shall be thrown down, and shall not be found anymore."*
>
> Revelation 18:2,8,21

Babylon fell in Old Testament times but wasn't totally destroyed. The spirit of Babylon is very much alive today and will not be deposed until Messiah comes again. Revelation 9 tells us more about these spirits:

> *Then the sixth angel sounded: And I heard a voice from the four horns of the golden altar which is before God, saying to the sixth angel who had the trumpet, "Release the four angels who are bound at the great river Euphrates." So the four angels, who had been prepared for the hour and day and month and year, were released to kill a third of mankind. Now the number of the army of the horsemen was two hundred million; I heard the number of them.*
>
> Revelation 9:13-16

Before the final battle, four demon spirits that are now bound in the River Euphrates that runs through Baghdad will be released and marshal an army of 200 million that will kill a third of the world's population—by today's standards that would be two billion people! Though the nature of these "horsemen" is not specified, I could easily see it being a terrorist army riding their suicide bombs to the destruction of ten times their number. And I can think of nothing that would more please the Saddams and Osamas of today.

In fact, biblical Iraq is even mentioned as a side in the final battle:

And they gathered them together to the place called in Hebrew, Armageddon. Then the seventh angel poured out his bowl into the air, and a loud voice came out of the temple of Heaven, from the throne, saying, "It is done!" And there were noises and thunderings and lightnings; and there was a great earthquake, such a mighty and great earthquake as had not occurred since men were on the earth. Now the great city was divided into three parts, and the cities of the nations fell. And great Babylon was remembered before God, to give her the cup of the wine of the fierceness of His wrath.

Revelation 16:16-19

Was America's war with Iraq a dress rehearsal for Armageddon?

When the final battle lines are drawn, Babylon will be on one side and Jerusalem on the other. Was America's war with Iraq a dress rehearsal for Armageddon?

Nebuchadnezzar Reincarnate

It should be obvious that the wickedness of Babylon—past, present, and future—is personified in Saddam Hussein, whose secret stockpiles of weapons of mass destruction threaten the entire world and whose violence, even to his own people, seems unquenchable.

Saddam has already used weapons of mass destruction on 200,000 Kurds. Because of his refusal to confirm the destruction of these weapons, Iraq was put under a U.N.-sanctioned oil embargo, resulting in monumental financial loss. He has given up $130 billion to $180 billion in oil revenues in order to protect his weapons stockpile.[1] This is the amount that he would have made off of his oil if he had simply complied with the U.N. resolution to destroy all of his weapons of mass destruction. But he didn't, and it is my belief that the reason we are not finding most of them is because he has moved them and his money out of Iraq into Syria and Lebanon.

Babylon has always opposed the Jewish people, and if Saddam Hussein survives—or one of his demon-possessed sons survives—I believe an attempt will be made to use his chemicals and biological weapons. We know he had them and I believe that some of them are in Syria and Lebanon, hidden along with his billions. His greatest joy is to live to fight another day and vent his demonic spleen on the U.S. in Iraq and Israel. (I believe that some of the Saddam clan are all ready out of Syria; many think they may be in south America, possibly Argentina—follow the money trail).

According to a *New York Times* article dated January 7, 2003:

"President Saddam Hussein of Iraq accused U.N. weapons inspectors…of spying on his country and, in a speech that summoned warlike images from biblical times, called on the Iraqi people to rededicate themselves to destroying their enemies. Saddam accused the United States of collaboration with 'the Zionist entity' Israel. [Author's note: The Arab world, refusing to recognize Israel as a nation, commonly refers to it as 'the Zionist entity' and the area of Israel as 'occupied lands.']²

"Saddam Hussein believes he is Nebuchadnezzar reincarnate and that he is destined to rule over a newly resurrected Babylonian Empire. One of the names of Iraq's elite Republican Guard units is the Nebuchadnezzar Division.

"Saddam has spent billions rebuilding the ancient city of Babylon, preparing to crown himself king and rule over an expanded Iraq. He has also spent enormous sums of money restoring many historical sites such as the Southern Palace of Nebuchadnezzar, the Processional Way, and the Ishtar Gate. It is said that he wants to restore Babylon as a symbol of his own greatness and intends to move his capital there.

"Since his defeat in the Gulf War in 1991, Saddam Hussein reportedly spent a billion dollars to build a palace on the site of ancient Babylon, featuring a plaque comparing himself to King Nebuchadnezzar. But more ominously, Saddam also spent billions on weapons of mass destruction, a threat to world peace."

What the World Was Never Told

After the Gulf War, U.N. officials gained access to a top-secret classified report. According to Kenneth M. Pollack, the principal official responsible for the implementation of U.S. policy toward Iraq for the National Security Council, "Saddam had pre-dele-

gated orders to Iraqi Scud units to launch missiles filled with biological and chemical agents at Tel Aviv if the coalition had
marched on Baghdad in 1991. His final act would be to rid the
Arab world of the Zionists."[3]

On December 23, 2002, Prime Minister Ariel Sharon said on
Israeli television, "There is a strong possibility that Saddam
Hussein has smuggled chemical and biological weapons into Syria
in order to hide them from United Nations inspectors."[4]

Israel's most respected military affairs commentator, Ze'ev
Schiff had predicted: "If Iraq strikes at Israel with non-conven-
tional warheads, causing massive casualties among the civilian
population, Israel could respond with a nuclear retaliation that
would eradicate Iraq as a country."[5] In other words, Bible
prophecy would be fulfilled and Babylon would be swept with
"the broom of destruction." Mark it down—this prophecy will be
fulfilled fully, but hopefully not in our lifetime.

In early December 2002, a ship that was bound for Yemen
from North Korea containing missiles was intercepted. Its cargo
was at first thought to have been legally purchased by the government of Yemen. The U.S. released the ship only after Yemen
agreed to keep the missiles themselves. It was later revealed that
the missiles' original ultimate destination was Iraq.[6]

It is believed that these weapons of mass destruction may be in
the hands of the terrorist group Hizbullah. Iraq has been shipping
long-range rockets through Syria into Lebanon for use by the terrorist organization Hizbullah.[7] Hizbullah has previously received
rockets via this route. There are now between 8,000 and 12,000
rockets in Lebanon with the ability to hit Israel's major cities.

The Syrian aid to Iraq also raises an important concern: As the
U.S. attempts to stabilize Baghdad, will Islamic terrorists regimes
and bordering states attempt to attack Israel and American
troops with weapons of mass destruction? We know Saddam had
them. Is it possible that he has already placed many in the hands
of terrorists? Why did America go to war with Iraq? I believe it
was because Syria was allowing Iraq to smuggle billions through
their country, including weapons of mass destruction. The U.S.
knew that Syria was literally joined at the hip with the Osamas

of the Middle East in Lebanon. Once these terrorists got their hands on WMDs, we would have no military target, just nut cases (sleepers) floating throughout the world. The Black Gold pipeline between Syria and Iraq was wide open prior to the war (a *quid pro quo*). America needed to end that quickly. Why? Iraq was feeding the sharks. How? Attack Iraq…fast!

Secondly, the U.S. needed a base to fight the war on terrorism. As President Bush said following September 11th, "We will take it to the terrorists." Now, we have a base.

Thirdly, Black Gold was used to finance the terrorist war that had to be stopped, not just in Iraq, but throughout the Middle East. Dictatorships in that region run their countries not by the ballot, but by the bullet. The Middle East alone has 22 dictatorships (family-owned corporations).

> *Democracy in Iraq could become as contagious as the ebola virus.*

Democracy in Iraq could become as contagious as the ebola virus. This would cause the last bastion of totalitarianism — the Arab regimes — to fall like a house of cards…similar to events in Eastern Europe and the former U.S.S.R.

American Special Ops in Western Iraq have been given the order to move on Syria. American soldiers in Iraq now have decks of cards showing the faces of 55 fugitive leaders of the Saddam regime. Saddam is the ace in the pack. The order has been given, "If there is 'credible intelligence' under the doctrine of 'hot pursuit,' then 'kill him, and get them.'"

In addition, there is a bounty out in the millions of dollars for Saddam. Dr. Germ, Missile Man, and dozens of his top leaders have escaped from Baghdad to Syria. Farook Hajazi, the former head of Saddam's secret police, is in Damascus. Mr. Hajazi is suspected of playing a key role in the plot to assassinate President George H. W. Bush when he visited Kuwait in 1993.

Expect a "head-fake." Syria will not go into a Saddam Hussein-type temper tantrum. They will, instead, play the diplomacy card to take the heat off them. When the heat is off, they will go back to running a terrorist-supporting regime. I believe that the Saddam clan will head for Lebanon or for South America...most likely Argentina. Ten billion dollars will buy a lot of favors.

Ten billion dollars will buy a lot of favors.

Isser Harel masterminded the capture of Adolph Eichmann, Hitler's butcher. Eichmann fled Germany to Argentina in 1946. On May 11, 1960, Harel captured Adolph Eichmann in Bueno Aires.

On April 15, 2003, *The New York Times* reported: President Bush declared today that "the regime of Saddam Hussein is no more," and his administration used America's rapid success in overthrowing the Iraqi leader to put new pressure on Iran and Syria, neighbors of the newly occupied nation. His statements...were part of a declared strategy to...reshape the Middle East, and Mr. Bush said he planned to make the new Iraq a model for democracy in the Middle East.

Zechariah 14:12 describes the severe circumstances the future holds for those who fight against Israel, and how seriously God regards the matter of supporting Israel.

> *And this shall be the plague with which the LORD will strike all the people who fought against Jerusalem:*
> *Their flesh shall dissolve while they stand on their feet,*
>   *Their eyes shall dissolve in their sockets,*
>   *And their tongues shall dissolve in their mouths.*
>
> Zechariah 14:12

This description of the plague on all nations who fight against Jerusalem, when people shall become as walking corpses, is a perfect description of the results of a nuclear attack.

Do you now see how the stage is set? If we are headed for the final battle and it will be between Babylon and Jerusalem, is the U.S.-led Coalition's war just a future echo of Armageddon or the first step on the road there? With the line drawn in the sand, on whose side will we ultimately end up? Remember, America liberated Afghanistan by providing the weapons, training, and money to defeat the Russians only to see it fall into the hands of Saudi-trained Islamic terrorists, thus forcing us to liberate Afghanistan again.

It is my belief that a critical time of choice is upon us.

"In doing God's work there is no substitute for praying. People of prayer cannot be replaced with other kinds of people — people of financial skill, people of education, people of worldly influence — none of these can possibly substitute for people of prayer."

E. M. Bounds

Some trust in chariots, and some in horses;
But we will remember the name of the LORD our God.

Psalm 20:7

What is all the commotion in the city? What is that terrible noise from the Temple? It is the voice of the Lord taking vengeance against his enemies.
Before the birth pains even begin, Jerusalem gives birth to a son.
Who has ever seen or heard of anything as strange as this? Has a nation ever been born in a single day? Has a country ever come forth in a mere moment? But by the time Jerusalem's birth pains begin, the baby will be born; the nation will come forth.

Isaiah 66:6-8 NLT

3

THE LINE DRAWN
IN THE SAND

*"We must never despair; our situation has been com-
promised before; and it changed for the better; so I
trust it will again. If difficulties arise, we must put
forth new exertion and proportion our efforts to the
exigencies of the times."*

George Washington

This line drawn in the sands of the Arabian Peninsula has been forming for quite some time. Since God first called Abraham out of Ur,[1] the sides have been forming. The whole world will soon have to choose—both nations and individuals—on whose side they will be. We must either choose Mount Zion (Jerusalem) and be among those who obey the voice of the Spirit of the Lord; or we will be left to the passions of our flesh, drinking "the wine of the wrath of her [Babylon's] fornication"[2]—the symbol of self-righteousness and idolatry. No one will be able to idly sit by and be neutral until the whole thing blows over (or blows up!). Those who would choose God's side will have to follow their choice with clear action and obedience to the voice of His Holy Spirit.

Get Out of Babylonia!

I mentioned before that the city of Ur from which Abraham was called was in modern-day Iraq. Just as Abraham was called out of physical Babylonia, we are being called out of the spiritual Babylonia of pleasing the flesh.

Now the Lord had said to Abram:
"Get out of your country…
To a land that I will show you.
"I will make you a great nation;
I will bless you
And make your name great;
And you shall be a blessing.
"I will bless those who bless you,
And I will curse him who curses you;
And in you all the families of the earth shall be blessed."

Genesis 12:1-3

The land Abraham went to was Canaan (v. 5), a land which includes modern-day Israel. Though we are called to a spiritual Israel and a New Jerusalem, God has never revoked His physical gift of the land of Canaan to Abraham and his descendants through Isaac. It was there that God made a covenant with him, saying:

"To your descendants I have given this land, from the river of Egypt to the great river, the River Euphrates."

Genesis 15:18

The size of the land Israel possesses today is one-sixth of 1 percent of the land possessed by the 21 Arab countries of the Middle East. While both groups are Abraham's direct descendants, God's physical promise was only to one of them. Thus the battle has always been between Abraham's two sons: Ishmael and Isaac.

Ishmael and Isaac

Abraham's descendants today include both Arabs and Jews, offspring of his sons Ishmael and Isaac. Ishmael was born to Hagar, the maid of Abraham's wife, Sarah. The Angel of the Lord appeared to Hagar and said to her:

"Behold, you are with child,
And you shall bear a son.
You shall call his name Ishmael,
Because the LORD has heard your affliction.

"He shall be a wild man;
His hand shall be against every man,
And every man's hand against him.
And he shall dwell in the presence of all his brethren."

Genesis 16:11-12

Few would disagree that this is a fitting description of the Arab terrorists with which we are afflicted today. Nevertheless, God made the following promise to Abraham regarding his son Ishmael: "I will…make a nation of the son of the bondwoman [Hagar], because he is your seed" (Genesis 21:13, author's insertion).

After Ishmael was born, Abraham's wife, Sarah, bore Abraham a second son, Isaac. It was to *Isaac*—and not Ishmael—that the covenant promises were passed: "In Isaac your seed shall be called" (v. 12).

> *God keeps His promises. He will have His way.*

The same blessing that was passed on to Isaac was passed on to his son Jacob. Jacob in turn passed the blessing on to his heirs, the patriarchs of the twelve tribes of Israel. That same blessing has been passed on continually through Isaac's lineage, all the way to the Jews of today. In other words, the *Jewish* people in particular are the ones that God said should receive special blessing.

> *I will establish My covenant between Me and you and your descendants after you in their generations, for an everlasting covenant, to be God to you and your descendants after you. Also I will give to you and your descendants after you the land in which you are a stranger, all the land of Canaan, as an everlasting possession; and I will be their God.*

Genesis 17:7-8

Regardless of the opinions of man and what the media says, God said the land of Israel belongs to the lineage of Abraham, Isaac, and Jacob. God keeps His promises. He will have His way.

Ishmael's Bitterness Is Turned to Counterfeit

To understand the force of the Islamic fundamentalist's world-view, we must backtrack to the birth of Islam. Muhammad, who was born in about A.D. 570 in Mecca, founded Islam. Muhammad was raised by his uncle and grew up working as a shepherd and camel driver.

Muhammad meandered with the trade caravans, exposing himself to the philosophical debates of the Middle East at that time. He also imbibed the teachings of Judaism, and the relatively new religion Christianity. These teachings made the young Muhammad dissatisfied with the traditional Arab polytheistic religion, with its many tribal gods.

Muhammad "retired" from the life in the fast lane of camel driving when he married a wealthy widow. Muhammad's new-found security allowed him to spend time in the desert contemplating and praying. One of these periods of meditation lasted six months, and climaxed with, according to Muhammad, the appearance of the angel Gabriel. Gabriel commanded Muhammad to "proclaim."

Muhammad had his commission to "proclaim." Now he needed some substance to bolster his proclamation. The period of revelation ensued. Over a span of some 23 years, "Gabriel" dictated the 114 suras, or chapters, of Islam's Koran, or holy scriptures, which are about the same length as the New Testament. According to Islamic teaching, the Koran is the decisive revelation of the divine will of Allah, superseding all previous revelations, including the Old and New Testaments.

Yes, it is true that the majority of Muslims are not terrorists in any form, but it is also true that the majority of Islamic fundamentalist hate everything the West stands for, and that hatred is so violent that it has birthed the terrorism that we fought in the streets of Baghdad. Our democracy and way of life is, in their eyes, a threat to their very existence. If the West prevails, Islamic women might vote and even drive cars.[3]

As amazing as this sounds, I had a Saudi prince tell me that if the troops had bacon with their eggs, it could mean the end of his regime. Permitting infidels on his soil was bad enough, but for them to bring their unclean ways was something that could not be tolerated. "Your people like bacon![4] This is a greater threat to our survival than Saddam," he said.

If the troops had bacon with their eggs, it could mean the end.

Mecca to Medina to Mecca

Muhammad realized that a religion is worthless without converts. His first disciple was his wife Kadijah. He won a few more converts, but Muhammad's proselytization success was limited. The commercial prosperity of Mecca depended on those who came to venerate the 360 idols that surrounded the holy "Black Stone" in the Ka'ba.[5] Muhammad struck at the pocketbook of the Meccans, thus instigating pervasive persecution.

On June 22, A.D. 622, the prophet fled to the city which became known as Medina, some 200 miles northwest of Mecca. The natives of Medina were more receptive to the prophet's teachings, and Muhammad soon had built a religious and political power base. However, the Jews in Medina refused to accept the new religion, claiming it had perverted the holy Jewish scriptures. Failing to convert the obstinate Jews, Muhammad resorted to what would become commonplace for the Muslims: He eliminated the Jews by slaughter and banishment. Muhammad set a sordid example for his present-day disciples: the Qaddafis, Khomeinis, Arafats, bin Ladens, and Husseins of this world.

Medina was a temporary refuge for Muhammad. His goal was to march on Mecca and avenge the earlier banishment from his hometown. When his force reached about 10,000 men, Muhammad marched on Mecca. He overthrew Mecca's defenders and seized the Ka'ba. The Ka'ba became the holy place of Allah, and Mecca the holy city of the Muslims, the spiritual center of Islam. Mecca is still a magnet for the Muslims. Muslims pray five times in the direction of Mecca each day and each Muslim is expected to make the pilgrimage [or haj] to Mecca at least once in his lifetime.

The Ultimate Prophet

After his takeover of Mecca, Muhammad began unifying the Arabian tribes into a new civilization. By the time of his death, most of Arabia had been consolidated under Muhammad. But Muhammad wanted more than just an Islamic grip on the Arabian Peninsula. He looked to Persia and beyond to bring his nascent religion. After all, Muhammad possessed the conviction that he had been called of Allah to reach the lost. Muhammad believed he was the ultimate prophet. Adam, Noah, Abraham, Moses, and Jesus, according to Muhammad, were also prophets. But Muhammad had the final word. He eclipsed all the previous prophets.

Interestingly, Abraham, the father of the Jews, is also considered the grandfather of the Arabs. Ishmael, Abraham's first son, became the father of the Arabs. Muhammad declared that since Abraham had submitted his first son, Ishmael, as a sacrifice,[6] that the descendants of Ishmael should be known as the sons of God. Thus, the assumption among Muslims that they are the "true" sons of God. They see the Jews as invaders, as they do the West. In their eyes the infidels are to submit to them, and it cannot be the other way around.

The Koran

At Muhammad's death in A.D. 632, the Islamic juggernaut was poised to strike at neighboring nations. But Muhammad did not just leave a legacy of an Islamic fighting machine. He also left the *Koran*, which means the "Reading," and consists of 114 suras which contain Muhammad's revelation. These suras are not arranged chronologically or topically, but according to their length—the shortest first and the longest last. Every Islamic father wants his daughter to marry the ideal Islamic lad: a fellow who can recite all 77,639 words of the Koran. Sometimes boys of ten or twelve are able to recite the entire Koran. Saudi Arabia exported the doctrine of Wahabism to Pakistan. Sometimes boys of ten or twelve are able to recite the entire Koran. They built schools and mosques. It was from those schools that those who became part of the Taliban were recruited.

To understand the Islamic mind-set, it is imperative to enumerate the fundamental doctrines of Islam, which are based on the Koran.

- The belief in one god, Allah, who rules the world.
- The belief in angels who do Allah's bidding.
- The belief in the major and minor prophets. Among the major prophets, Muhammad listed Adam, Noah, Abraham, Moses, and Jesus—and of course, himself, the final prophet. He taught that every country had a national or local prophet.
- The strong belief in the Day of Judgment. True believers were to be rewarded in paradise, a "garden of delight." Unbelievers would suffer the torture of the Seven Terrible Hells.
- The belief in determinism. Muslims believe nothing happens in the world unless Allah wills it, including September 11th.

The Five Pillars of Islam

What must a Muslim do to enter the blissful "garden of para-dise"? Islam embodies five stringent tenets that all good Muslims must heed. In carrying out these five tenets, many Muslims display a fervor lacking in many Christians. Tepid Muslims are as disdainful to Allah, according to Islamic teaching, as lukewarm Christians are to Christ.

The following are the Muslim's "Five Pillars of Faith":

1. Confessing with heart and lips the *shahada:* "There is no god but Allah and Muhammad is his messenger."

2. Saying five daily prayers while bowing in the direction of Mecca. The worshipper is to pray standing, bowing down, prostrating, and sitting. Prayers are to be offered in the morning before sunrise, just after midday, late afternoon, at sunset, and at night. (Incidentally, the refusal by the Jews to bow down in the direction of Mecca infuriated Muhammad. Instead, the Jews prayed in the direction of Jerusalem, in the direction of the Temple Mount.)

3. Muslims are expected to fast 28 consecutive days every year during the month of Ramadan. A fasting person cannot eat, drink, smoke, or engage in sex from dawn until dusk, although he can do these things at night.

4. Every adult who is physically and financially able is to make a pilgrimage, or *haj*, to Mecca at least once in his life.

5. Islam requires that every believer give a portion of his earnings to charity. Omar II said: "Prayer carries us halfway to God, fasting brings us to the door of His palace, almsgiving lets us in."

Islamic Law

In addition to the Koran and the basic tenets of Islamic faith, the followers of Muhammad have developed a complex code of ethics, morality, and religious duties. The teachings explicitly explain even the most mundane matters of conduct.

One of Muhammad's written works contained a code of behavior that was said to be "a rigorous, minute, specific codification of the way to behave in every conceivable circumstance, from defecation to urination, to sexual intercourse, to eating, to cleaning the teeth."

Like the governments it has spawned, Islamic law is authoritarian. According to Islamic law, thou shalt *not* engage in: frivolous pleasures, singing and playing of musical instruments of any kind, gambling, the use of liquor, slander, lying, meanness, coarseness, intrigue, treachery, disloyalty in friendship, disavowal of kinship, arrogance, boasting, obscenity, aggressiveness, and tyranny.[7]

No matter how noble these principles, however, following them would no more lead to righteousness than the laws of the Old Testament—human desires and selfishness were still in the way. Because of this, Islam was soon turned from a path of liberation and devotion to a means of controlling others. Islam turned to the "law of the sword" that exemplified Muhammad's first major conversions.

Jihad was born.

Christianity Versus Islam

Christianity differs from Islam as day differs from night. Whereas the Bible admonishes the followers of Christ to "turn the other cheek," the Koran, the Islamic handbook, urges adherents of Allah to "make war on those who believe not...until idolatry is no more and Allah's religion reigns supreme."

> *Christianity differs from Islam as day differs from night.*

We only have to look at the inception of Christianity to distinguish the basic difference between the two religions. The appearance of the Messiah was foreordained before the formation of the earth. The Old Testament gave precise references to the appearance of the Messiah. Therefore, there was no great surprise when the angel Gabriel appeared to a young Jewish lass some two thousand years ago announcing the birth of the long-awaited King of Kings. Gabriel's pronouncement fulfilled hundreds of Old Testament prophecies. Christianity had its origin in the heart of God.

"Prayer is of transcendent importance. Prayer is the mightiest agent to advance God's work. Praying hearts and hands only can do God's work. Prayer succeeds when all else fails."

E. M. Bounds

4

JIHAD: A TRULY
UNHOLY WAR

*"Oh people of the book,
do not go beyond the bounds in your religion and
do not say about Allah anything but the truth.*

*"There is no God but Allah
He has no co-partner.
The messiah, Jesus, son of Mary,
is but a messenger of Allah and His word
which he cast upon Mary and a spirit from Him.*

*"So believe only in Allah and of his messenger but do
not say three (trinity) and it will be better for you.*

*"Allah is only one God
far be it from His glory that He should have a son.
Verily the religion in Allah's sight is Islam."*

Translation of an inscription in Arabic
from the wall of The Dome of the Rock Shrine
The Temple Mount Site, Jerusalem

Where conversions by the sword replace persuasion and the
seeking of truth, Islam turns from its lofty guidelines to the
law of the bullet, militancy, treachery, terrorism, and violence
between Islamic factions as well as toward all non-Muslims.
These brutal Islamic concepts can be traced back to Muhammad's
writings in the Koran that urge the waging of *jihad*, or holy war,
against all non-Muslims. As holy war was an integral part of
Islam at its onset, so it remains to this day.

The Koran's admonition to wage holy war is clear. The Koran
contains such statements as, "Make war upon those who believe
not...even if they be People of the Book (that is, Christians and

Jews). Make war on them until idolatry is no more and Allah's religion reigns supreme."[1]

Islamic scholars have even concocted a dogma for holy war, based on the Koran's teachings. The scholars contend it goes against Islamic law to retreat from *jihad* and adopt peace unless the Islamic force is weak and the opponent is strong. After renewed preparation to wage *jihad*, the Muslims can reconvene the hostilities.

According to Islamic law, *jihad* will never cease—it will last to the Day of Judgment. War forms the basis of relationships between Muslims and their opponents unless there are justifiable reasons for peace; i.e., when the opposing force has more firepower.

Islamic Imperialism

From the start, Islam realized success with its "conversion by the sword"[2] policy. Muhammad blessed those "converts" who accepted Islam peaceably. But to those who rejected Islam, Muhammad sent word that, "I, last of the prophets, am sent with a sword. The sword is the key to Heaven and hell; all who draw it in the name of faith will be rewarded."[3]

Muhammad, and later his followers, first unsheathed their swords in the regions adjoining Arabia. Twenty-five years after Muhammad's death, Muhammad's disciples had captured and forcibly converted Persia, Syria, Palestine, and Egypt. In less than 75 years the Muslims had swept through Northern Africa. They crossed the narrow Strait of Gibraltar and entered Europe through Spain. Only Charles Martel's crushing defeat of the Islamic forces at the Battle of Tours in A.D. 732 stemmed the furious Islamic onslaught.[4] Almost one thousand years later, in 1683, the Polish king John Sobieski thwarted the marauding Muslim Turks at the gates of Vienna. Yes, the Muslims had come within a hair of dominating Europe, the continent whence our Christian heritage came.

But the menacing Muslims had entrenched themselves firmly in the Mediterranean world. Islam's sphere of influence stretches from the Atlantic Ocean to the borders of China—an expanse covering the territories of all the great empires of past history. Today, there are 44 Islamic states; half of these are Arab. There are about one and a half billion Muslims worldwide, about one-fifth of the world's population. Muslims cover half of the globe, from Northern Africa to Southern Russia, from Northern India to Indonesia. The non-Muslim world also has a distinctive Islamic flavor. There are about 24 million Muslims in Europe, a million just in Great Britain. British Prime Minister Tony Blair, America's strongest ally, pressured President Bush all through the Iraqi war to push "The Road Map" plan (see chapter 10 and Appendix A for more information on this). Is there any wonder that Tony Blair needs an Israeli *quid* for a Palestinian *quo?* There are two million Muslims in France. Should there be any wonder why the French were against war in Iraq? More than a million Muslims live in Germany, so here too, should

> *The Islamic world had blazed brightly for a time on the world stage.*

we wonder why Germany also was against war in Iraq? There are also roughly 80 million Muslims in Russia. There are more than one billion Muslims represented at the U.N.—is it any wonder that three of the four members of the Quartet represent the majority of the Muslim world? Can you imagine if the number were reversed and all Jewish that there might be a conference held to demand that an Arab country give Jews land for their own state?

When Charles Martel quashed the Islamic onslaught in Europe in the eighth century and the Christian Crusaders launched their courageous but foolhardy mission to recover from the Muslims the holy places of the Holy Land, the Muslims turned to the defensive. Later, the Turks, Mongols, and Tartars attacked the Islamic bastion in the Middle East. Though these invaders converted to Islam, the Muslims of the Middle East were too busy fending off and converting the invaders to wage an aggressive holy war. Furthermore, Muslim infighting allowed no time to wage *jihad* against the infidels. Though the Islamic world had blazed brightly for a time on the world stage, Europe began to emerge from its darkness about 550 years ago, thus eclipsing the burned-out Islamic meteor. The Muslims still had the will to wage jihad, but not the means.

Collaboration

Throughout the 13-plus centuries of Islamic existence, the Islamic world has relied on a disparate lot of collaborators to destroy the Jews through holy war. The Jews have been persecuted wherever they have wandered. Europe proved to be especially inhospitable to the Jews. Spain virtually liquidated all Jews during the Inquisition of the 15th century. Just about every European country has allowed anti-Semitism to rear its ugly head, from Italy to Estonia.[5]

During the later Middle Ages, Poland became a haven for the Jews. By the beginning of World War II, 3.3 million Jews lived in Poland. Today, only 6,000 Jews remain in Poland. Hitler killed three million Polish Jews. The post-World War II communist government finished the job that Hitler began. In the 20th century, Germany has been singled out as the sole persecutor of the Jews. In all, Hitler killed six million European Jews, but in many countries, including France, Romania, the Baltic countries, and Russia, his purging of the Jews met widespread approval. For centuries Satan has coerced people to loathe God's Chosen People.

Today, there is another international power allied with the Islamic world that is wholeheartedly committed to eradicating the Jews in a frighteningly unholy holy-war alliance. That great power is the former Soviet Union. Russia has had a long and dreadful history of anti-Semitism. The remnant of Jews, about 1.6 million, remaining in Russia and its former republics today faces daily harassment, and repeated denial of exit visas. The Soviets and

Muslims make strange bedfellows—an avowedly atheistic nation aligning with a fanatical religious group. The Soviet-Islamic bond is held together by one thing: their hatred for the Jews. The Arab world united behind Hitler in World War II and great numbers still teach to this day his demonic doctrine that the Jews are responsible for all the world's problems. In that Christians worship a Jewish Messiah, they too are a problem that must be dealt with. The battle is a spiritual one and it is all over a *Jew* not the Jews!

Black Gold

The Muslims could be infuriated until their turbans tattered, but resentment alone could not help them wage a successful jihad without the modern-day weapons of war. The jihad of the Muhammadan era is impossible today. Holy war can no longer be fought by Muslim warriors astride sturdy camels, their razor-sharp swords glistening in the scorching desert sun, with cries of *"Allah-hu-Akbar!"* (Allah is Almighty!) piercing the still air. No, 20th and early 21st century wars are fought with bombs, machine guns, bazookas, mobile missile launchers, hand grenades, and tanks. But where would these poor Muslim desert dwellers get the money to finance modem war? Unbeknownst to even the Prophet Muhammad, the Muslims had been treading for hundreds of years atop the petroleum reserves which would finance their war chest in the 20th century.[6]

The very ascendancy of the West paved the way for the reemergence of the Islamic world. The West began its climb to the top of the world heap with the onset of the Industrial Revolution in the late 18th century. The inventions and techniques of the Industrial Revolution allowed the United States and Europe—the "West"—to become the dominant actors on the world stage—that is, when they weren't pummeling each other in war.

After World War II, relative tranquility returned to the Western world, and the United States, Western Europe, and an Eastern upstart, Japan, surged above the other nations of the world in the realm of economics and technology. But it was a cheap source of energy that propelled the West to attain technological and financial superiority. That source was petroleum—and the Islamic countries possessed (and still do possess) a disproportionate reserve of the black gold that makes the world run.

Islamic Blackmail

Throughout the 1950s, 1960s, and early 1970s the United States and the Western world continued to run their factories and cars on inexpensive oil. America produced much of her own oil and Europe purchased oil at sand cheap prices from the Middle East. But in the 1960s American oil production began to lag and by the early 1970s the United States had become a net oil importer—with just about all of the foreign oil coming from the Islamic countries.

However, the Muslims didn't deal their slick oil card until their disastrous defeat when they attacked the Israelis in the 1973 Yom Kippur War. How well I remember filling up my gas-guzzling car with gasoline selling at 26 cents a gallon. But then came the OPEC oil embargo in the autumn of 1973 and double-digit gasoline prices became as rare as snow at the equator.

The Arab oil-producing countries finally realized they had the West's head in a noose. The oil price escalations induced a worldwide recession. Prices for petroleum, goods made from petroleum such as plastics, and goods produced by petroleum skyrocketed. But while the industrialized nations reeled under excessive oil payments, the coffers of the Middle East oil sheikhdoms overflowed with the West's hard currency. Not only did the Muslims begin to exert tremendous pressure on the West to disassociate themselves from Israel, they also received massive sums of money to finance holy war around the globe—mostly directed at Israel. Sticks and stones wouldn't break Israeli bones, but bombs and blackmail would. The West, in particular Western Europe, stood by idly, first as the OPEC producers put a figurative gun at its head, and then as the Muslims put real guns to the heads of Israelis and those countries that support Israel—especially America.[7] President Bush considers Iran, a terrorist state, to be in an axis of evil. Iran is presently attempting to build a nuclear reactor with the help of the Russians. They say it is strictly for domestic use to provide energy. There is only one problem with that argument—Iran is the number three oil-producer in the world. They do not have an energy problem. In addition, America buys oil from Iran in the same way that America was buying oil from Iraq. Buying Iraq's oil was, regretfully, helping to finance a terrorist regime which violates the Bush Doctrine on terrorism. Obviously, that will not happen anymore. I also believe that America will stop buying oil from Iran now that the U.S. has broken OPEC's Black Gold cartel by controlling Iraq's oil.

Holy War Rekindled

In the last century we have witnessed a resurgence in the Islamic quest to wage holy war. There are a number of reasons for this. The Muslims have felt humiliated by the emergence of the West as *the* world leader. But the overriding factor that has united the Islamic forces for holy war in the Middle East was the rebirth of the nation of Israel in 1948. This was the greatest catastrophe in the eyes of the Muslim world.

The Islamic dictators in the Middle East needed an enemy in order to justify an army, and someone to blame for the human misery in their poverty-stricken nations. Israel was the perfect choice, in that the Arab world already had Hitler's conspiracy theory from World War II. Muslims condoned a Jewish presence in the Middle East before 1948, but they were not ready to allow the Jews to repossess territories that had been in Islamic hands no matter how small a period of time in Jewish history. Add to this the humiliation of millions of Muslims losing on the battlefield to a woefully out-manned Jewish fighting force.[8]

The renascent Israel has served as a catalyst to give the Arabs and the wider family of Islam some sense of unity. The Muslims are willing to overlook their mutual mistrust in order to destroy the nation of Israel. Muslims could withstand the Middle Eastern involvement of the Turks, Mongols, Tartars, French, and British, but a reborn Israel—which has no intention of leaving—has raised the Islamic world's indignation to a fevered pitch. In their eyes a Jewish State is an "Act of War" against Islam. But to them, Israel is still the "Little Satan," whereas America is the "Great Satan," and both are attempting to destroy their way of life. They do not hate America because of Israel; they hate Israel because of America. The battle is over a Book—one that both the Jews and the Christians believe: the Old Testament. If it is right, then the Koran is wrong.

> *To them, Israel is still the "Little Satan," whereas America is the "Great Satan."*

"A great civilization is not conquered from without until it has destroyed itself within."

Will Durant

O GOD the Lord, the strength of my salvation, You have covered my head in the day of battle.

Psalm 140:7

5

A FURTHER
DISTORTED ISLAM

---

*"The ruling to kill the Americans and their allies —
civilians and military — is an individual duty for
every Muslim who can do it in any country in which it
is possible to do it."*

From a Fatwa (an Islamic decree or teaching)
issued by Osama bin Laden
February 23, 1998[1]

This chilling "teaching" by the man believed to have orchestrated the World Trade Center and Pentagon attacks is based upon the most murderous and misguided version of Islam: Wahabism, from the Wahabis tribe in Saudi Arabia. The Wahabis themselves had been branded heretics in hundreds of Fatwas issued by mainstream Muslims. Despite this, however, it has taken root among enough Muslims to become the greatest threat to America and the rest of the world since the danger of nuclear annihilation posed by the Cold War.

Wahabism began as a movement propagated by warrior-preachers in the 18th century. It interprets the Koran in its most literal form and is the most uncompromising, fundamentalist type of Islam. For many centuries, it was a relatively small sect, mainly among the one tribe from which it derived its name — the Wahabis — and was generally dismissed by all other Muslims as heretical — until it struck oil. Lots of oil. The Wahabis were insignificant Bedouin nomads on the Arabian Peninsula until the British, in the early 20th century, elevated them to prominence to help take control of Mecca and Medina — and some oil fields.[2] The combination of religious power through control of Islam's holiest sites and sudden economic power through oil wealth has given the

Wahabis tremendous sway over the Muslim world. Now they rule Saudi Arabia and are responsible for the growing politicization of Islam that has suddenly emerged to threaten the entire world. Through their influence, Wahabism has become the backbone of the beliefs of Osama bin Laden and terrorists like him and of their hatred of the West. It is the doctrine that lights the fuses of all of the suicide bombers.[3]

One year after the terrorist attacks on the World Trade Center and the Pentagon, I was asked by *The Jerusalem Post* to write an Op-Ed in reflection on the changes in the world since those attacks. Strangely, it seemed appropriate to me to discuss the impact of Wahabism. The article ran as follows: (I mentioned the story of Yigal Carmon at the beginning of the book, but I feel it bears repeating)

Islam and the Infidels

September 4, 2002

On the morning of February 26, 1993, Yigal Carmon, then counter-terrorism adviser to Prime Minister Yitzhak Rabin, warned the Pentagon that radical Islam was an imminent threat to America. At the end of his briefing, smirking critics told him that they did not consider a religion to be a threat to national security. I was shocked as Yigal told me this story in Jerusalem—he went on. Later that morning Carmon flew on to New York, where, while having lunch, a huge explosion took place nearby: Islamic terrorists had attempted to blow up the World Trade Center, killing six people and wounding 1,000.

Last September 11, Islamic terrorists finished the job. No one wants to admit why Americans were attacked, just by whom they were attacked. But Osama bin Laden is only the vanguard of a religious hatred that originates in the Kingdom of Saudi Arabia and seeks to impose the will of radical Wahabi Islam throughout the world. The terrorist threat that bin Laden demonstrated on September 11 was just the opening salvo in the first world religious war of the 21st century.[4]

An earlier campaign in the same war began in Israel in 1987, called the *intifada*. From mostly stone throwing, this violence has escalated into the horrific suicide bombing that has come to characterize the so-called *"Al-Aksa intifada."*[5]

From scenes of Palestinians dancing on West Bank rooftops during Iraqi Scud attacks of the Gulf War, we are now witness to Palestinian mothers celebrating and handing out sweets upon hearing that their sons have blown themselves up killing innocent Israeli bus passengers. In this grotesque dance of death, Islamic zealots who are murderers are revered as religious martyrs.

On December 9, 1987, the Muslim Brotherhood met and issued a communiqué calling for the intensification of the Palestinian uprising. Representatives of the Islamic Resistance Movement signed it. Abdullah Azzam, Osama bin Laden's mentor, developed the theme: "There is no solution to the Palestinian problem except jihad." The goal was simply to export Ayatollah Khomeini's "Islamic revolution" via the Hamas movement, and thereby islamicize the Palestinian national struggle. Just as Islam had defeated the strongly pro-Western shah of Iran and shamed America, and just as Islam had defeated the communists in Afghanistan and led to the collapse of the Russian empire, so would the "Zionist entity" be slowly bled to death—and so would the Great Satan, America.

There were no expressions of outrage from leading Muslim clerics on September 12—a silence as deafening as that regarding Jews who are slaughtered weekly in Israel by the same type of Islamic terrorists. This same silence has greeted the deaths of Palestinians themselves, who were branded as collaborators and summarily executed for allegedly working for Israel. Just a couple of weeks ago, Ikhlas Yasin, 39, the mother of seven children, was shot and killed by executioners of Fatah's Aksa Martyrs Brigades in the main square of Tulkarm.[6] An intolerant, radical Islam is striving to become the vocabulary of everyday life, reshaping the language of politics, culture, and traditions, and taking no prisoners.

WHY HAS America not succeeded in numerous attempts to implement a peace process between Israelis and Palestinians—not in Madrid, not at Camp David, not in dozens of public and secret peace initiatives? The simple reason is that radical Islam does not negotiate with infidels; and if not with the Great Satan, then surely not with the Little Satan.

U.S. President George W. Bush has stated that he found it "strangely coincidental" that every time the U.S. attempted to move toward peace there was a massive terrorist attack in Israel. But there is nothing coincidental in such attacks, for they are aimed both at murdering Israelis and at the same time humiliating the Great Satan. The only thing American brokering has done is weaken its greatest ally in the Middle East and open the floodgates to an ever more aggressive Islamic terrorism. When you reward Islamic terrorists with political or economic concessions, they can only assume that you fear them and that crime pays.

The last thing that corrupt and shaky Arab dictators want is peace between Israel and the Palestinians.[7] Their regimes are sustained by military power and they know they cannot justify having an army without an enemy. Without the Jews to blame for their poverty, illiteracy, and lack of democratic freedoms, their populations would turn on them, as did those of Eastern Europe and the former Soviet Union.

Rev. Franklin Graham, who prayed at Bush's inauguration and at the September 14 memorial service in Washington, said in his book, *The Name:* "The United States is engaged in a war against terrorism. But this war has a unique twist for Americans. We are not fighting to stop Hitler or godless Communism.... Those who have attacked America invoke their God's name, Allah."

Radical Islam has given birth to a weapon that truly cheapens human life: the suicide bomber. But this will be as nothing compared to the weapons of mass destruction under preparation in Iraq and other radical Islamist states; weapons whose targets may begin with Israel but ultimately are aimed at the world's greatest democracy.[8]

Well, those critics aren't smirking anymore. Until the events of September 11, America could afford to look benignly at some of the modern manifestations of Saudi Wahabism. One harmless example was the two Saudi princes who accompanied NASA astronauts on a space shuttle flight a decade ago. Their mission was to give official witness before a Wahabi religious court that Earth is, indeed, not flat.[9] Back on the ground, however, the Saudi Wahabis have waged a consistent, dedicated campaign to transform Islam from a religion into a totalitarian political ideology.

Islamic fundamentalism will be the greatest challenge to the democratization of Iraq. (Iraq's population is 60 percent Shiite.) Under Saddam, Shiite Muslims attempted to establish an Islamic state. He countered that threat with assassinations, arrests, and severe curbs on their freedom. They were not allowed to make pilgrimages to their holy cities of Karbala and Najaf for Ashura ceremonies that included men whipping themselves with chains. These rights are an expression of mourning for the sect's leader, Hussein, whom they believe was the grandson of the prophet Muhammad. He was killed by rivals in Karbala in 1680.

The Islamic clerics are already preaching a strict adherence to Shariah, the Islamic legal code based on the Koran. In their minds, democracy is a threat to Islam and an invention of infidels. There is little wonder that there are no real democracies in the Middle East, except Israel. And, that is why, after the U.S. freed Afghanistan from Russia, the nation became 10 times worse under an Islamic fundamentalist perceived theocracy, who assumed control.

Already, the Shiite clerics of Iraq are demanding an Islamic State...a state where the Koran defines good and evil, not the "infidels"...where young girls are circumcised, where women cannot vote or drive a car...where televisions, and even dominoes, are not allowed.

In their minds, they are on a mission from God, an opportunity to "seize the moment," and restore pride to their humiliated people. The clerics believe that Islam, the only religion of Allah, was given to the first man, Adam, who was the first prophet of Allah. They believe it is the religion of all true prophets sent by Allah to mankind. According to Islam, "Abraham was not a Jew, nor a Christian; but an upright Muslin." (Soorah Aal'imraan 3:67.)

America prides itself on freedom of religion, and in the separation of Church and State. In the eyes of the Shiite clerics, that is blasphemy. In the eyes of Allah, both the Church and State are Islam. Freedom of religion cannot be tolerated. All religion must submit to the "true religion (Islam.)"

This is the reason that moderate Saudi Arabia does not allow a church on every corner...or any corner. The Islamic states in the Middle East, and for that matter the world, will attempt to spark an Islamic revolution in Iraq, if not with the bullet, then with the ballot. Either way, they are not going to accept a secular state.

That would be as outrageous as the war in the eyes of the Iraqi "Minister of Misinformation."

There will be a call for another "Operation Iraqi Freedom" with Islamic fundamentalists fighting for the minds and bodies of Iraqi citizens. Remember, the Taliban were Wahabists, as were the 19 homicide bombers of September 11th, as is Osama bin Laden.

Wahabist clerics will flow into Iraq faster than oil. They will be financed by Islamic states, and why not? If democracy succeeds, then the outrage will begin, and the game of living like kings will be over. Islamic Shiite clerics will be as determined to establish an Islamic state in Iraq as their brothers were in Iran. Nothing must hinder their dream! This will be a major problem for the U.S.

"Where's the Outrage?" was the title of another article I wrote for the *Wall Street Journal*. It was about Arabs who were killed by the P.L.O. in the West Bank for selling property to Jewish settlers. That was six years ago and nothing has changed. The Palestinians are still P.L.O. pawns!

The "Sword of Oil"

Today, Saudi Arabia and its ruling families are an international financial giant. Starting in 1973 Saudi Arabia, as the leading oil-producing OPEC country (the Soviet Union actually pumps the most oil each year), began to unsheathe its "sword of oil." This sword has been trimming the financial fat off the West for the last few decades. With its vast oil revenues Saudi Arabia has improved the standard of living at home, but they also hold an incongruous measure of strength abroad for a desert kingdom with a population of only 10.4 million. Above all, the Saudis have used their newfound wealth to spread their beliefs and use it to create pockets of power around the world. Though the Saudis sell themselves as moderates, they are immoderate in the aid they give to radical Arab states and terrorist groups, as America found out on September 11th.

The striking paradox about Saudi Wahabism is, however, that although it is home grown, it is aimed exclusively for export to certain key areas of the world. In mosques and Islamic centers throughout the world are former students who were given free tuition at Medina University in Saudi Arabia and now expound Wahabi doctrine. This doctrine in effect denies traditional practices that have been handed down from father to son for some fourteen hundred years.

The true believers of Wahabism who are exported by Saudi Arabia are saying that the Islam practice for fourteen hundred years—until the Wahabis—was all wrong! The reason why the Saudis are careful to encourage Wahabism only outside the Arabian Peninsula is self-preservation. It is why they exiled Osama bin Laden and why he was hiding in Afghanistan, for it does not take much imagination to picture what would happen to the extravagant Saudi royal family if an Arabian version of the Taliban took over.

Nor is the export of Wahabism by any means random. Its strongest centers are in Pakistan, Afghanistan, Albania, Algeria, Daghestan, Tajikistan, and Uzbekistan. Except for Albania, all are oil pipeline routes in potential competition with the Gulf. And Albania, for its part, is in a very key area geographically linking the East with the West.

Initially this campaign appeared to be succeeding. The Saudis, in an effort to help stem the spread of godless communism, helped create a new force in Afghanistan—the Taliban. The Taliban militia captured 80 percent of the country's territory and, for a while, succeeded in bringing stability to the region. Simultaneously, it helped reduce the influence of American antagonists Russia and Iran on the frontier of oil-and-gas-rich Central Asia.

Some of the practices of the Taliban were grim illustrations of how far Islamic teachings had been distorted and imposed by this fanatical dictatorship. Nowhere in the Koran or the Sunna (the teachings and practices of the Prophet Muhammad) does it say that women should cover their faces and hands, or that women cannot work, or that the beard must be long, or that men must be beaten for not praying publicly, or that women must be kept locked in their homes. Jihad is purely and simply the worst kind of murder—no matter what your beliefs or religion. The distorted teaching has boomeranged to threaten world peace, not to mention the true interests of all Muslim nations in achieving progress for their citizens.

The Wahabi teaching on martyrdom takes the hatred it engenders to the next level and this is the mind-set that the West cannot understand. Perhaps we can get our thoughts around the supposed promises of this self-sacrifice: that they will be granted eternal life, a crown of glory before Allah, 72 virgins as their concubines, and there holy blood will atone for the sins of 70 of their relatives exempting them from the horrors of hell. Yet even if we in the West believed our self-sacrifice would bring us these rewards, would we do it? Personally, I don't think so. What we don't understand is the process of indoctrination—the lies—that are told these pawns in the hands of their teachers from the time that they are small children. The lies and false promises that are told them by their parents and relatives. The day-in, day-out promises of bliss and supreme ecstasy that they will experience at the moment of the blast that will kill them and as many others as possible. The way they make it sound, you would think it was some kind of extreme sport instead of what it actually is: murder and a one-way ticket to the hell they were promised they would escape.[10]

...you would think it was some kind of extreme sport instead of...murder.

While the political threat of Wahabism has been flaunted perhaps most blatantly by the Taliban in providing refuge to bin Laden and his closest followers in Afghanistan, its hatred and willingness to murder indiscriminately regardless of the cost is also reflected in the almost daily atrocities committed by Hamas and Islamic Jihad against Israel, to cite just two of the fundamentalist organizations that receive Saudi support. Since September 11,

most of the non-Islamic world have come to see Islamic fundamentalism as holding it hostage via a diabolical combination of
terror, dogma, and the willingness to be killed to kill. This threat
is, of course, perceived most poignantly by Americans who fear
correctly that the forces of evil represented by bin Laden are still
poised to strike—perhaps worse than before. This "cult of the
suicide bombers" has stripped the face from war and put it on the
person sitting across from you on the bus. It has taken our daily
routines and made them a gauntlet of fear. With the feeling that
they could strike anytime, anywhere, we can become crippled
more completely than if they just took out a gun and shot us.

The Power of Petrodollars

Saudi Arabia is not the only Muslim country to use its oil wealth
as leverage in world affairs. Petrodollars (the name given to the
currency the West pays to the oil producers) proved the downfall
of the Shah of Iran. The Shah wanted Iran, the Persia of the Bible,
to become the Switzerland of the Middle East. He wanted to mod-
ernize a country where the inhabitants lived in the same fashion as
their forefathers lived in the time of the Bible. The Shah's plans
failed when Islamic fundamentalists wrested power away from the
Shah. The Shah's descent led to Khomeini's ascent—a disaster for
America and the Middle East. The Muslim Brotherhood of Iran
exported their revolution, their fundamentalist beliefs, and their
methods to Palestine. The Islamization of the Arab population in
Israel twisted the mind of an entire generation, convincing them
that martyrdom is a greater glory than compromise.

Petrodollars have harmed the Muslim states as much as they have
helped them. Is the war in Iraq about oil? It had better be, as Harel
told me, "Oil buys more than tents." If seizing the assets of terrorism is a way of stopping them, how much more is seizing the
commodity that created those assets? Iraq is number two behind
Saudi Arabia in oil reserves. Giving the world a more ready
access to such a commodity could well cut off not only OPEC's

stranglehold on the world, but also greatly reduce the petrodollars they can amass to keep terrorism alive and growing. A despot or dictatorship could be ignored, but not one with billions of petrodollars to export and augment terrorism.[11] These dictators are worried sick most of the countries are nothing more than family owned corporations that run their governments off the bullet not the ballot. Their greatest fear is democracy and losing control of OPEC terrorist-supporting states that could lose trillions of dollars if the valve is opened wide in Baghdad. They know that President Ronald Reagan defeated communism with the economic stealth bomber. They also know that bomber is now in the air. This is the first time a neighbor was in the neighborhood that was not willing to use black gold to fund terror and was able to beat the other neighbors with their own weapon. The last bastion of dictatorships could go the way of Eastern Europe and the former U.S.S.R. if they play the "I support terror" game.

The two greatest weapons in the Islamic war chest against Israel and the West are the vault and the valve. Every week that passes places the nations of the West more and more at the mercy of the Arab League because of their petrodollar-filled vaults and their stranglehold on the shut-off valve to the flow of oil. We are seeing the evolution of a type of jihad that might be termed econoconflict. As one analyst aptly noted: "What the Arabs failed to do with their tanks and troops, they are attempting to do in boardrooms and brokerage houses. They are continuing to battle Israel by applying pressure on its allies—without ever firing a shot."

A Little History

The Organization of the Petroleum Exporting Countries (OPEC) was created in Baghdad on September 10-14, 1960. OPEC became one of the most powerful forces in the world because of two events—two oil embargos against the West.

The first was in 1973 when OPEC triggered an Arab oil embargo and the Arab states vowed they would drive Israel into the sea. They told the Arabs in Israel to fight or leave and after they defeat her they could come back—which was really the spark that ignited the Palestinian crisis. Then they attacked Israel and lost.

The second was in 1978 at the outbreak of the Iranian revolution. Oil prices increased and the Arab oil states became a political and economic force as they had never been before in the modern era. It was also the real beginning of their covert financing of terrorist organizations.

Personally, I believe that the days of OPEC blackmailing the West have ended, along with OPEC's ability to use black gold to finance terrorism thanks to a very courageous President George W. Bush.

However, the Islamic world still wants to bring Israel and the West to their knees, either by the sword or with financial muscle. What they can't gain militarily or through terrorism, they will try to gain through blackmail. It's a blackmail that Israel has resisted, but which proves tempting to the West. No matter what the new world order offers the United States in return for its disassociation from Israel, the Bible says that God will bless those who bless Israel. Will God bless or curse the United States? The answer depends on whether we support or disavow Israel. God is not a promise breaker!

Red-Hot Flames

To review, there are three main reasons why the flames of Islamic jihad flicker so brightly in our present time, and why Wahabism has found such fertile soil in which to plant hatred and terrorism:

1. The Islamic world resents the preeminence of the Western world. At one time the Islamic/Arab world was the center of culture and science, but in recent centuries the Islamic world has become a cultural and scientific backwater.
2. The Islamic world resents the rebirth of Israel, probably the only single event that has pulled the Muslims together into

some semblance of unity. The Muslims hate the Jewish state. Jihad participants say they will not cease their struggle until Israel "disappears." Without an enemy, there is no one to blame except rich Arab dictators.

3. The Islamic "sword of oil." Petrodollars have given their ill will away. What the Islamic world cannot accomplish militarily, they will try to achieve through economic leverage. As long as petroleum remains the most important fuel in the world, the Islamic oil producers will be able to fill their treasure chests with more petrodollars. The Muslims will attempt to blackmail the West into disdaining Israel. They will also use their petrodollars to finance a terrorist jihad against Israel and the West—and what the West spends on one "smart-bomb" can pay for hundreds if not thousands of suicide bombers.

Those in rule have learned many things in these centuries of jihad, not least of which is protecting their own interests and using others as pawns to take the risks that will ensure they remain in power. Direct, personal conflict is only one way of conquest, but if I can send my "brother" to fight for me, so much the better—and I will gladly pay his way and supply his weapons.

The Saudi Wahabis have mastered this new style of "jihad behind the boardroom doors." They have bred an insane death-cult with Modern Islam as its Trojan horse. On one hand they negotiate and sell oil to their enemies as if they were friends, while with the other they take the money from those transactions and feed it to the terrorists who murder those same enemies or use it as economic power to further their visions. In this way they stay away from the tip of the spear and the edge of the sword, and keep their hands relatively clean. After all, their pawns will draw enough blood for all of them.

Trust in the LORD with all your heart,
And lean not on your own understanding;
In all your ways acknowledge Him,
And He shall direct your paths.

Proverbs 3:5-6

6

THE SWORD'S EDGE:
THE PALESTINIAN LIBERATION ORGANIZATION

"Hitler first killed Jews, then he killed Christians.
Our culture and our democracies are the root of [the
terrorists'] rage. If we're right, then they are wrong."

Isser Harel
Founder of the Israeli Intelligence Agency, Mossad[1]

Although most Arabs would like to do away with Israel, no group is so vocal and in the spotlight as the Palestinians and their terrorist organization, the P.L.O., led by Yasser Arafat. He is the primary voice behind the familiar "land for peace" mantra. Their primary goal is the formation of a Palestinian state through the eradication of Israel.

The Palestine National Covenant

The Palestinian Liberation Organization was first organized in Cairo in 1964 (three years before the 1967 Six Day War) under Egyptian Arab League auspices. They called their official document the Palestine National Covenant, since the word *covenant* conveys a holier connotation than *charter* or *constitution*.

This document has been revised several times, but still contains twenty-three articles that reject the Balfour Declaration (the 1917 document that supported the formation of the nation of Israel in Palestine by the Jews), the 1947 U.N. Partition Resolution dividing Palestine into Jewish and Arab states, and the Jews' biblical claims on the land of Israel. Most importantly, they deny the Jewish right to be a nation and a free people. They insist, instead, that all the territory properly belongs to the Palestinians and that only those Jews living in Palestine prior to the "Zionist invasion" (which most of them date to the time before the Balfour Declaration) can be regarded as legitimate Palestinians and thus allowed to stay. Despite the lengthy rhetoric, the covenant essentially calls for the physical eradication of Jewry and the State of Israel in order to establish a Palestinian state in place of both Israel and Jordan.

The P.L.O. in Jordan

Things began in earnest to change after the Six Day War in June of 1967. Around the time of this war, the *Fatah* (The Movement for the National Liberation of Palestine) headed by Yasser Arafat, began to take control of the P.L.O. Arafat maintained his base of operations in those days in Jordan, as had his predecessors in the P.L.O.

King Hussein had welcomed them warmly, but they repaid his welcome by intrigue and treachery within Jordan itself. They invited the Bedouins to join their ranks and oppose the king. They erected roadblocks to harass the citizens and collect fees from them, and they terrorized the Palestinians within Israel's borders to intimidate them into embracing them as their leaders in the call for the liberation of Palestine.

Please note that the P.L.O. claims to represent the Palestinians, but in fact does not. The largest percentage of Palestinians are Jordan citizens not Israeli citizens in that Jordan attacked Jerusalem and they left! Furthermore, the P.L.O. appointed *itself* to this task. No election was ever conducted among the Palestinians to establish a body to represent them to the world. The original appointments were made by the representatives of the Arab League, none of which were democratically elected.

In any event, the P.L.O. continued to tax King Hussein's patience (and people!) while they enjoyed the refuge of his country. They nearly established a rival capital for Jordan at Karamah, a few miles north of the Allenby Bridge over the River Jordan. From there they exchanged artillery fire with the Israelis. Fearing Israeli retaliation, Hussein tried in vain to stop it. The P.L.O. ignored him.

Israelis Fight Back

In 1968, the Israelis finally fought back, warning civilians to evacuate Karamah. That alerted King Hussein who dispatched 48 tanks, eleven artillery batteries, and two brigades of infantry, but not until after the Israelis had reached Karamah.

Approximately 320 members of the P.L.O. were involved. The Israelis surrounded and destroyed al-Fatah installations, killing about 200 terrorists and taking the remaining 120 prisoners. But, as they withdrew from Karamah, they met Jordanian troops and the battle was on.

Twenty-six Israelis were killed and 70 were wounded in the fighting. They also lost a considerable number of armored vehicles. Arafat escaped to the town of Salt on a motorcycle, whereupon al-Fatah declared a great victory on Radio Amman, complete with dancing in the city streets.

The terrorists decided to stay in Amman, and King Hussein really had trouble on his hands. They roamed the streets of the city brandishing their weapons and defying local police. Amman became a scene of virtual anarchy.

Hostages Taken

Finally, in June 1970, King Hussein ordered his troops to drive the P.L.O. — or Fedayeen (those who sacrifice themselves) as they like to call themselves — out of the city. In the bloody fighting that followed, the terrorists murdered Major R. J. Perry, military attaché to the U.S. Embassy in Amman. Then they occupied two hotels — the Intercontinental and the Philadelphia — and held 32 American and European guests hostage.

With that, George Habash—the General Secretary of the Popular Front for the Liberation of Palestine (PFLP), which was also part of the P.L.O. at this time—announced they would kill the hostages and blow up the hotels if the Jordanian troops didn't back off. Habash and Naif Hawatmeh—the leader of another P.L.O. subgroup, the Democratic Front for the Liberation of Palestine (DFLP)—both received funding from the Soviets. They could afford to attack an Arab head of state.

Since Arafat's money came from the Arabs, he sought to be more conciliatory. Nevertheless, the fury of the confrontation pushed Arafat more and more toward Habash and Hawatmeh.[2] (Arafat is the Blockbuster of the Middle East. Instead of paying a few dollars to see a video, he is paid millions. Nothing does more to arouse the masses than seeing an Arab house destroyed. Of course, no one is ever told that the demolished houses were hiding places for terrorists who were blowing up Jews.)

On June 12, 1970, Hussein did back off after another one of Habash's speeches threatening to kill the hostages. After that things were quiet, but tense. Then in September the violence began again when Habash's men hijacked two jumbo jets (Swiss Air and TWA planes) and brought them to Jordan's Dawson Field. Three days later, on September 9, they hijacked a British Overseas Airways Corporation jet and brought it to Dawson too.

Altogether they had 445 hostages whom they threatened to blow up in the planes if imprisoned terrorists in Israel and Europe were not released within seven days. By September 12, all but 54 of the hostages had been freed. Arafat, speaking for the central committee of the P.L.O., endorsed Habash's PFLP demands.

Finally, on September 16, over Radio Amman, Hussein announced a military government to restore order to his troubled land. The next morning he unleashed the Bedouin Arab Legion in a full-scale operation against the P.L.O. Tanks demolished every building in Amman from which there was firing. Before Hussein was finished, he had killed around 3,000 Palestinian terrorists and broken the P.L.O. power in Jordan.

Hussein's action prompted an immediate reaction from Jordan's northern neighbor, Syria. Men and equipment poured over the border to reinforce the terrorists. Syrian commandos struck and captured two Jordanian border villages on September 18, and Hussein stiffened for all-out war with Syria, which greatly outnumbered him in tanks and aircraft.

Israel and the United States mobilized their forces, giving notice to Syria that if she launched a full-scale invasion, she would encounter more than Jordanian troops. It worked. Syria held back and the Jordanians were able to drive the P.L.O. out of their country.

Lebanon: A Microcosm of "Holy" War

From Jordan, the P.L.O. moved on to Lebanon, the only Arab nation with a significant Christian—Syrian Orthodox and Catholic—population. When the French discontinued their mandate of Syria and Lebanon in 1946, the Christian majority in Lebanon worked out a delicately balanced arrangement with the Muslim minority under a democratic constitution. Results were happy enough, and Beirut became a bustling and prosperous commercial center whose citizens probably enjoyed the highest per capita income in the Middle East.

When Palestinian Arabs fled Israel during the 1948 war, several thousand were admitted to Lebanon—not more lest the Christian-Muslim balance of population be seriously disturbed. Disturbing that balance was always a matter of grave concern, especially to the Christians who stood to lose the most. They had felt safer from Muslim antagonism under the French and had been reluctant to see them go.

All the while, the Lebanese Muslims argued for unification with Muslim Syria. They did not have much regard for Lebanon's pre-Islamic past, the days of the Phoenicians, and the enormous wealth of Tyre and Sidon. For them, all significant history commenced with the advent of Islam around A.D. 632 and so the tension brewed beneath the surface.

The Palestinians decided to disturb the Christian/Muslim balance in Lebanon and did so out of proportion to their actual numbers. That was because agents of the P.L.O. worked actively in the refugee camps and established bases within them from which to launch terrorist attacks into Israel.

The Lebanese government was faced with a dilemma: to drive the P.L.O. out would anger the Muslim population, yet to let them stay would enrage the Christians. Therefore the Lebanese prime minister denied their existence in public and negotiated with Arafat to limit raids into Israel so as not to provoke Israeli reprisals. This arrangement, however, worked only briefly, until the P.L.O. in Lebanon commandeered an El Al airliner. The Israelis promptly dispatched jet fighters to Beirut's airport where they destroyed Arab airliners on the ground.

While Lebanon was thus knocked off balance, its Muslim neighbors applied pressure to secure for the P.L.O. the sole right to supervise and police the refugee camps in southern Lebanon. In addition, the Lebanese were persuaded to release P.L.O. terrorists whom they had imprisoned for their subversive activities against the Lebanese government.

Consequently, terrorism inside Lebanese borders revived. On November 15, 1970, to cite but one example, terrorists surrounded a house, apparently at random, in the town of Aitarun. It was occupied by Mahmoud Faiz Murad, his wife who was in her ninth month of pregnancy, and his father. All three were gunned down in cold blood when they resisted the terrorists' attempts to remove them by force.

The Lebanese Muslim community sided with the P.L.O. and, in 1975, civil war erupted between the Christians and Muslims in that country. Christian apprehensions were expressed by several spokesmen. Dr. Albert M'khebar, a member of parliament, declared, "I will renounce my Lebanese nationality, acquire an Israeli one, and go around the whole world to proclaim my apostasy from the Arabs and Arab nationalism if its true nature is what we see in Lebanon."[3]

Raymond Edde, head of the Christian National Bloc Party in parliament, complained, "The Western world no longer is concerned with the defense of the Christians in Lebanon."[4] *Time* magazine carried this statement by Elis Marvun of Beirut:

> Now I can understand why Israel is refusing the suggested "democratic Palestine" where the Israelis and the Palestinians would live together. The outstanding example the Palestinian people are giving now in Lebanon is, I believe, more than enough to warn Israel of such a trap…. I am a Lebanese citizen whose brother and two cousins have been coldly shot down by the Palestinians in their homes in a Hitlerian style. I can already see the day when, in order to survive, our people will join Israel."[5]

As fighting between Muslims and Christians intensified, the President of Lebanon, Suleiman Franjieh, publicly announced the following about the Palestinians:

> The Lebanese had given them a refuge, and our reward was the destruction of Lebanon and killing of its people. I have served the Palestine cause for thirty-five years. I never expected the day would come when I would ask God to forgive my sins because I serve a people who did not deserve to be served or supported.[6]

Official appeals for help were made to the United States and the United Nations, both of which remained aloof while Syrian-trained and Soviet-equipped troops of the Palestine Liberation Army poured across the border from Syria into Lebanon. They were accompanied by regular Syrian troops.

The net result was a near takeover of Lebanon by Syria. That was the situation that finally precipitated Israel's invasion of Lebanon in 1982. Meanwhile in southern Lebanon, the leader of the Lebanese Christian Army, Major Saad Haddad, established an enclave in which the Lebanese people in that region could dwell in relative safety. Haddad and his troops tangled frequently with P.L.O. terrorists moving from camps in his area toward the Israeli border.

An Extraordinarily Brave Man

Once while I was in Israel I went to see Haddad. I had been to Lebanon once before, in 1972. Then I had visited Beirut, a beautiful, peaceful city. A taxi driver had talked at length about how Lebanon was one of the most beautiful resort spots of the Middle East. What a contrast with today's devastation.

My visit with Major Haddad took place inside Israeli territory, in Metullah to be exact, late in September of 1980. I told him there were some who considered the Israelis to be involved in the terrorism of southern Lebanon.

Haddad looked sad and said: "I would like them to come here and see who is controlling the area. Then they will know that the P.L.O. terrorists are making the rules. The south has become a big base of terrorists. If we are shooting, it is to defend ourselves against these terrorists. For five years we have been cut off from all sides, except the south. The P.L.O. wants to exterminate our people and nobody cares."

"Have you captured many of the P.L.O. Arabs?" I asked.

Haddad's eyes narrowed seriously. "Do you think I'm fighting Arabs on the front line? Far from it. I'm fighting terrorists from all over the world. North Korea, Cuba, South America, and just a month ago, two Czechs got killed in a fight. The P.L.O. has people from almost all the communist countries and from all the Arabic Islamic countries too—Libya, Iran, Egypt. These are the P.L.O. your State Department is supporting. Your country, the Europeans, and all the Arab countries support them."

"Why do you think we support them?" I asked.

"I'll tell you why. The terrorists are frightening the rich Arab countries, so they give the P.L.O. money, as much as they want, because they are desperate to keep them away from their country. Then the rich Arab countries turn around and put pressure on America and Europe to say the P.L.O. is good or something like that.

"But they are not good! They are criminals. Look at Lebanon. It used to be a paradise. They burned it. They killed a whole country.

And they want to destroy the whole Middle East. They have said many times that they consider all the old regimes as reactionary, and they are going to make progress by making them communist.

"That's why they don't attack Israel from Jordan anymore. The Syrians won't allow them either, unless they are in Syrian uniforms. The Jordanians stopped them in September of 1970. That's where they got the name Black September. Only Lebanon allows them. Why? Because Lebanon is a weak country, and it has a Christian President that the P.L.O. wants to get rid of.

"The Christians of the world should wake up and help their brothers in Lebanon. If the Christians in Lebanon are exterminated, so will all the other Christians in the Middle East. The large Christian population of Lebanon is what guarantees the safety of the Christians in other Arabic countries.

"And what the terrorists have done here in southern Lebanon they will do to churches wherever they go. People should see what has happened to the villages in southern Lebanon that the terrorists have occupied. They ruin them. They are making a toilet of Lasherish [one of the towns in southern Lebanon occupied by the P.L.O.]. And they would do the same to Jerusalem if they got their hands on it. They would turn the churches into mosques."

"What about the U.N. forces north of you?" I asked. "Are they helping to keep peace?"

"The U.N. is doing nothing. They are just there for show. Worse than that, sometimes they are covering for the P.L.O. The area where the U.N. troops moved into used to be clean of P.L.O., but not anymore. The P.L.O. moved in and they have camps inside the U.N. area from which the P.L.O. makes terrorist actions.

"They came from there to one of the villages and planted mines. Four people were killed in that village. And last night, at exactly eight o'clock, they fired rockets from Dar Amish, which is in the U.N. area. If we trusted the U.N. forces to protect us, we would all be dead. We have to count on ourselves."

"What about Israel?" I asked.

"That's the only country that cares for us. Without Israel we would have been exterminated a long time ago. Four of the main Christian villages were almost completely wiped out by the terrorists. In El Damour there was a terrible slaughter. They just lined up the little children and killed them all. Can you imagine that?

"We are not ready to face that. It must not happen to our children and our families. That is why we are so thankful for Israel. They are supposed to be our enemy, but they are helping us."

Land for Peace!

It was sometime around this time (1969 to 1973 or so) that the CIA created a secret liaison with the P.L.O. in the hope of stopping them from murdering American diplomats and military personnel overseas. That dangerous liaison continued both officially and unofficially until 1988 when open negations with the P.L.O. began and once Arafat had said the magic words, "I denounce terrorism."

The sinister alliance started back in 1969 when Robert C. Ames, an American CIA agent, first made contact with Ali Hassan Salameh, founder of Arafat's Force 17 security guards. On November 3, 1973, Deputy CIA director Vernon Walters met officially with Salameh to hammer out an agreement with the P.L.O. The terms of the agreement were that the P.L.O. would not kill any more U.S. diplomats and in return the U.S. would eventually recognize "Palestinian rights for a homeland." In other words, the first "land for peace" agreement was cut promising Israel's land to the Palestinians without Israel even being consulted.

It was another decade before the *Wall Street Journal* broke a story on the C.I.A./P.L.O. agreement bringing it to the attention of the American public for the first time.[7]

"But Arafat Seems So Sincere"

One of the greatest tricks of the 20th century was the transformation of Yasser Arafat from a demon to a diplomat in the public eye—and the United States is the one who pulled it off! President Clinton courted Arafat more often than any single foreign visitor. In fact, America has all but bought and paid for Arafat's "land for peace" philosophy. Despite the change in public opinion, however, Arafat and his methods have never changed. A quick evening of research will show you that Arafat has remained a terrorist from the time he took over Fatah until today, often even personally approving attacks, all the while denouncing terrorism in public and deflecting blame to radical renegade groups acting on their own initiative. There are many examples of Arafat revealing his true terrorist nature, but I will leave you with just this one.

On February 12, 1986, forty-seven senators sent a letter to the U.S. Justice Department demanding the indictment of Yasser Arafat for the brutal murders of Ambassador Cleo Noel and *charge d'affaires* C. Curtis Moore in Khartoum, Sudan.[8] Nothing has been done yet—but there is no statute of limitation on murder. One chilling piece of evidence incriminating Arafat is an audiotape of him giving the order to have the American diplomats killed. Virginia Congressman Eric Cantor pointed out that the State Department is still in possession of this audiotape.[9]

If Yasser Arafat is as sincere about ending terrorism as he says he is, there are several things he must do before he turns himself in for murder:

1. An official end to the *intifada* (the Palestinian uprising against Israel) that has been the fertile soil for encouraging terrorism;
2. an end to the teaching of "glorious" martyrdom in the territories;
3. an official commitment to honor the extradition requests for all terrorists who have killed Americans and all foreigners, including Israelis;
4. the dismantling of all terrorist organizations, including the removal of *Hamas* and *Islamic Jihad*—both of which are groups on the U.S. terrorist black list—from his cabinet.

When coupled with the U.S. and Israel jointly monitoring and a reasonable timetable, peace is achievable. Without this real attempt to dismantle terror, however, Arafat and the P.L.O. will indeed remain an obstacle to peace at best, and an insane justification for terrorism to the Islamic world at worst.

Why discuss the P.L.O. in a book about the U.S. and Iraq? Consider the fact that while the U.S. is embroiled in its war of terrorism, our government is at the same time pushing for a Palestinian state for these terrorists! The P.L.O. is a group that has done nothing but terrorize our friend and ally Israel from behind a charade of diplomacy.

Remember, the P.L.O.'s terrorism activities have not only affected Israel, but the entire world. Democratic presidential candidate, Robert F. Kennedy, was shot at point-blank range by Palestinian terrorist Sirhan B. Sirhan on June 5, 1968. Kennedy died the following day. President Bush wouldn't negotiate with the terrorist Taliban government, why should Israel negotiate with the terrorist P.L.O. while they dance in the streets when Americans were killed in Iraq and sent the P.L.O. bombers into Baghdad through Syria? What does the P.L.O. have to do with the war in Iraq? The anti-American, anti-Semitic Muslim media and their ministers of misinformation have convinced its masses that the U.S. is the Khmer Rouge and Baghdad is the killing field.

Never was there a more important time for moral clarity and for God-fearing people everywhere to rise up! If America chooses to side with the very terrorists we say we are out to eliminate, we can only welcome more attacks within our borders in an ever increasing magnitude—a sure guarantee that the war on terrorism will be a very long and protracted ride on the back of the terrorist tiger.

For Zion's sake I will not hold My peace,
And for Jerusalem's sake I will not rest,
Until her righteousness goes forth as brightness,
And her salvation as a lamp that burns.

Isaiah 62:1

7

A BLOOD-SOAKED HISTORY; A BLOOD-SOAKED FUTURE

> *"My brother and I will fight my cousin. My cousin and I will fight a stranger."*
>
> Arab saying

B aghdad's butcher, Iran's Islamic bullies, and Syria's card-carrying terrorist bulwark, testify of a malevolent manifestation of a religion conceived in the pit of hell. Just about every Westerner recognizes the names of these diabolical Islamic leaders. The acronym OPEC has become a rancid morsel of alphabet soup for the West and a constant reminder of our oil dependency on the Islamic world. We read about the Islamic world every day in our newspapers. We recognize the interplay of the Islamic world with ours, but we fail to realize that Islam is more than a religion; it is rather an all-embracing system—a code and pattern of life, including political, economic, and legal matters. And even more importantly that religion can kill and threaten the survival of a free society. September 11th was indeed a "Wake-up Call from Hell."

One of our biggest mistakes, however, is to see them as unified. Their holy war is not just limited to indiscriminate Islamic attacks against Israel and the United States. The 44 Islamic states may hold the common bond of Islam, but religious similarities do not translate into friendship and trust.

Iran and Iraq

For example, Iran and Iraq don't just dislike each other; they hate each other with a vengeance. The 1980-1988 Iran-Iraq war has left an estimated 500,000 Iranians killed or wounded and an estimated 300,000 Iraqis killed or wounded. Many of the Iranian casualties were teenagers who died in human-wave "martyr" attacks against entrenched Iraqi defenders. All Iranian soldiers go to war with a "key to heaven" around their necks, guaranteeing automatic entry into Islamic bliss if they die in battle. Children have been tied together by their hands, keys to heaven placed around their necks, a red martyr badge stuck on their clothing, and marched into the fields to clear mines.

Iran's Ayatollah Ruhollah Khomeini had termed the conflict a "holy war." The war began over a disputed island, but there are deeper reasons for the war than territorial acquisition. The Iranians are predominantly fundamentalist branches of Islam; the Iraqis are Sunni Muslims, more liberal and numerous in the Islamic world. Khomeini would like to export Iranian-style revolution abroad, and neighboring Iraq is a great place to start. Another interesting difference: Iraq is Arab, Iran is Aryan. (The Iranians are descendants of the Aryan/Sumerian peoples, also referred to as the "black-headed, or dark-haired people.)

The Unifying Power of a Common Enemy

Despite their hatred of one another in the past, however, Iran will stand by its distant cousin Iraq in opposing the U.S., as will Syria, Jordan, and other Arab states, even if only behind boardroom doors. Despite the fact that the U.S.-led Coalition forces are coming as liberators, Arab states will not be able to tolerate either the Western influence or democracy that these liberators will bring with them. Though none of these countries can afford to openly defy the military firepower of the Coalition forces, they have not been slow in bussing their "citizens" across the borders to help their cousins fight the strangers.[1] It seems very likely that once we think the war is over, that then the real bloodshed will begin. Terrorism in the Bible Land will not end with the fall of Baghdad, but will rise to a new level. Israel will insanely be blamed and efforts will be made to "punish" the Jews, as they are the closet target and the most vulnerable.

Every possible attempt will be made to create a civil war in Iraq. The greatest danger for the troops will come after the war for Baghdad is ended, and American troops have to begin the long struggle of stabilizing the country. It may appear to be going well for a while, but there is no question that Islamic vengeance is as systemic as the flu, and more contagious; but more importantly, it is also extremely patient as we found out on September 11th, 2001. They waited eight years before attempting to blow up the World Trade Center again after their blotched attempt in 1993—and Saddam had more weapons of mass destruction and money than Osama ever dreamed possible. You can be sure that, if he is alive, the blood trail of his money and even weapons of mass destruction stockpile will lead from Syria to Lebanon and beyond. They will attempt to find safe havens, and become "sleepers" until the heat dies down.

In late March of 2003, an Israeli general told me that one nod from Saddam—or one of his demonic heirs—could begin a world terrorism crisis unlike any that has been seen before, and as invisible as a stealth fighter jet and many times more deadly. While the U.S. spent millions shooting off one of its "smart-bombs" to hit a target, fundamentalist terrorist groups could send a sea of their "H" human bombs in an effort to accomplish equally precise bombings.

Islam's Deadly "H" Bomb

On Saturday, March 29, 2003, a seemingly harmless orange and white taxi traveling near Najaf in central Iraq refused to turn around at a U.S. Army roadblock. The search for weapons led one soldier to order the trunk opened. In the next instant everyone was dead. The driver of that taxi had pledged a vow of martyrdom, believing that by doing so he would be granted eternal life, a crown of glory on his head, and 72 virgins in paradise, and that 70 of his relatives would be exempt from the horrors of hell by his vow to shed his own blood in order to shed the blood of Islam's enemies. This was the first such attack to kill Coalition troops, and it took place on the eleventh day of the war in Iraq. The bombing killed four soldiers from the 3rd Infantry Division. The trunk was booby-trapped to detonate the bomb; the blast blew a crater in the ground.

Only a week later on Saturday, April 4, 2003, a car pulled up near a U.S. checkpoint northwest of Baghdad. From the passenger side, a pregnant woman stepped out, screaming in fear. As three Coalition soldiers rushed to help her, the car exploded, killing the woman, the driver, and the three soldiers.

I was in Mogadishu in 1993. An American Black Hawk helicopter was downed in the center of town. A roughly 20-hour firefight ensued in which 19 U.S. soldiers and over a thousand Somalis were killed. Shortly after this President Bill Clinton made the decision to pull out of Somalia. The terrorists considered that a glorious victory.

I was also in Beirut in 1983 when a truck bombing killed 141 U.S. military personnel. Two terrorist attacks took place that year: one in April and another in October. The result was that President Ronald Reagan pulled U.S. forces from Lebanon and—to the shocked amazement of Israel—demanded that Israel not kill Yasser Arafat and allow his 10,000 terrorists to leave Beirut for Tunisia.

This is the jihad's "H" bomb—the terrorists' "smart bomb"—that our Western mind-sets have yet to recognize or comprehend—human beings willing to sacrifice their lives for the glory of murdering others. We still cannot accept that fact that the religion of Islamic fundamentalism (Wahabism) can kill. These "Human" bombs give their lives willingly believing that they will be received into paradise as martyrs because of the corrupt teachings of their leaders, but when they wake up in the afterlife, it won't be God the Father who greets them. They have been deceived, and the consequences are not only gruesome and devastating for those who are left to care for their victims on earth, but are eternal for the misinformed bombers themselves.

The Weapon that Chased America from Lebanon

The portent of an Islamic "H" bomb is the most ominous sign of holy war. They started most notably in Lebanon when they attacked Israeli forces, the U.S. Marines, and American Embassies. The carnage began on April 18, 1983, when a car bomb exploded outside the U.S. Embassy in West Beirut. Sixty-three people died, including 17 Americans. Islamic terrorists gleefully claimed credit for this gutless attack. The reason for the attack: Islamic extremists wanted to send a message to the United States to stay clear of Israel. The Muslims claimed that the United States was a pawn of Israel, an assertion that is ludicrous. The brutal attack hammered home this Islamic axiom: *Any* friend of Israel is an enemy of ours. The truth is the pawn has always been Israel. She has done more to help the U.S. than all of the Arab countries combined and is the last firewall between the "H"-Bomb and the West!

When the United States sent peacekeeping forces to Lebanon in mid-1983, the Islamic world rose in unison to denounce "American meddling and imperialism." But where was the Islamic world in 1970 when P.L.O. leader Arafat, evicted from Jordan by King Hussein, moved his retinue of rabble-rousers into Syria and then was shown the door and headed to Lebanon.

When the U.S., French, British, and Italian peacekeepers entered Lebanon in 1983, they arrived with noble intentions: to end a messy war that was originally started by the P.L.O. The Western forces were prepared to fight hand-to-hand to stop the bloodletting in Lebanon, but instead they never saw the faces of the people who came to kill them. Even their training in guerrilla tactics did little to help them understand an enemy that fought with terrorism and suicide bombers.

The West's idealistic intention that they could undo centuries of hate in a matter of months shattered in the early hours of Sunday, October 23, 1983. The Marines at the U.S. Marine headquarters near Beirut International Airport were getting their last winks that day before the familiar "up and at 'em" would arouse them from Sunday slumber. Instead of a bugle sounding, though, a deafening explosion rocked the headquarters. Muslim extremists, bringing to land a page from the Japanese kamikaze pilot handbook, had driven a truck bomb into the compound and destroyed the barracks. A truck laden with explosives and driven by a member of Islamic Jihad roared past the startled Marine guards and rammed into the Marine headquarters. The bombing killed 241 U.S. servicemen, while the driver of the bomb-filled vehicle supposedly earned automatic entry into Islamic paradise for his selfless sacrifice. I was in Beirut at the time and can tell you first-hand that holy war is everything but holy.

A few other Islamic terrorists realized their "greater glory" simultaneously with their brother bombers at the U.S. Marine headquarters. The same grisly performance also took place at a French military barracks. Fifty-eight French paratroopers were killed. This was no ordinary Sunday of morning worship for the French and Americans, but a full day of Sunday mourning.

> *This was no ordinary Sunday of morning worship for the French and Americans, but a full day of Sunday mourning.*

Overall, America, not France, was the favorite target in Lebanon for terrorist organizations. There was a violent instant replay of the April 1983 bombing of the U.S. Embassy annex in East Beirut on September 20, 1984. This time a van chock-full of 350 pounds of explosives blew up 35 people from the Embassy. One more suicidal, holy-war warrior entered Islamic bliss—this time killing 12 "infidels," including two American servicemen.

Same Tactics; New Century

This is precisely what the world of terrorism will hope to accomplish in Iraq. There will be an enormous escalation of suicide bombing attempts. Before the war Saddam promised a new house and cash for every Palestinian family who would sacrifice a child to blow up Jews, having pledged over $50 million toward this cause. The P.L.O. to honor Saddam built a memorial in Jenin to honor the first Suicide bomber. He and those like him won't hesitate to use the same tactics again.

Captain Andrew Valles of the First Brigade, a civil and military affairs officer, responded as most of us would to the taxi explosion of March 29, 2003: "I don't know what motivated this guy to kill himself."[2] The truth is, it is estimated that approximately 10 percent of all of those who practice the Muslim religion believe in this form of "martyrdom"—not as a form of suicide, because they don't believe they are killing themselves, but as a glorious sacrificing of their lives for Allah. Iraqi TV said of the suicide attack by this taxi driver, "It is the blessed beginning; he wanted to teach the enemy a lesson in the manner used by our Palestinian brothers."[3]

In February 2003 before the war in Iraq began, Osama bin Laden urged Iraqis in an audiotape on Arabic television that they should employ the tactics frequently used by the Palestinians against Jews in Israel if the U.S. invaded their country. In response to the first suicide bombing of the war, Iraq's Vice President, Taha Hassin Ramadan, said, "The attack was not the work of a freelance fanatic, but part of a coordinated effort to beat back the invasion." He went on to say that these suicide bombings are the weapon of choice, and would eventually also take place on U.S. soil. "We have bombs that will kill 500 people, but I am sure the day will come that a single martyrdom operation will kill 5,000 enemies. This is just the beginning. You will hear more pleasant news later."[4] This suicide bomber, in a special service, received a special commendation from Saddam Hussein and a posthumous promotion to colonel.[5]

America has won the war against Iraq. However, there is another threat that the West must fight that will follow that: A new generation of human bombs infuriated by our victory. That bomb might be a man or a woman, a teenage boy or a teenage girl, a pregnant woman or an old man waving a white flag of surrender—anyone in a car, anywhere.

The key is the human heart and the human spirit.

The aftermath of the conventional war in Iraq will be a terrorist war. Iraq's future will be more of a Mess then Messianic. Every video showing dead Arabs will increase the Muslim resistance until the stakes of these suicide bombers will rise in an attempt to outdo each other.

Saddam's Real Threat: Suicide Bombers Armed with Weapons of Mass Destruction

There is no question that Saddam Hussein possesses weapons of mass destruction. It is no surprise that the battle for Baghdad is becoming a holy war. The call to arms comes from Islamic clerics preaching in mosques to the masses and firing them up with distorted images seen on Arabic television, justifying their extremism by misinterpreting the Koran through the eyes of Wahabism. They will urge their brothers and sisters to strike the infidels, meanwhile more than 25 percent of the mosques in the U.S. follow the Wahabist doctrines. American generals can indeed win the war for Iraq with smart bombs and even kill Saddam and drive his partners in crime out of Iraq, but they cannot kill the demons behind them, nor can they drive those demons out of the country. Only those who understand the power of prayer can do that. Otherwise these demons will just find another home to dwell in.

"When an unclean spirit goes out of a man, he goes through dry places, seeking rest, and finds none. Then he says, 'I will return to my house from which I came.' And when he comes, he finds it empty, swept, and put in order. Then he goes and takes with him seven other spirits more wicked than himself, and they enter and dwell there; and the last state of that man is worse than the first. So shall it also be with this wicked generation."
Matthew 12:43-45

Thus the call to spiritual warfare and battle is not hopeless; indeed the key is the human heart and the human spirit, which as much as it is the root of their rage, it is also the place of transformation through the wonder-working power that operates in the realm of the unseen. All battles on earth are first won or lost in the heavenlies before their results are felt on earth.

No longer do terrorist-harboring states need nuclear reactors to produce the deadly material necessary for atomic bombs. It can be produced in centrifuges the size of washing machines.[6] The most massive inspection would never find it. America's war with Iraq is the beginning of a war against state-sponsored terrorism and the U.S. wants to fight it with tanks and guns and missiles in their territory or ours. The U.S. will go after the entire network of terror—the regimes that support it and the organizations that harbor it—and the policy will be preemption. No longer will America be too late to intercept another September 11th—if we can help it.

Israeli intelligence is concerned with the possibility that terrorists, after pledging to give their lives as suicide martyrs, will inject themselves with smallpox, or expose themselves to SARS, then mingle with people in greatly populated areas. Slowly dying, they will go about in crowds, breathing on people. They will become biological H-bombs (human bombs). Without the power of prayer, the world will be left with a marching army of human corpses dispensing the plagues of the book of Revelation, but through the power of prayer a revival like the world has never seen can truly sweep the planet and transform hatred into hope.

> *Without the power of prayer, the world will be left with a marching army of human corpses dispensing plagues.*

The Spiritual "H" Bomb Brings Life, Not Death

The power of prayer is greater than the greatest war strategies, global-satellite-guided precision strikes, and the greatest 21,000-

pound "Mother of All Bombs" combined, and is *the* most effective weapon against any level of terrorism. America dropped two MOABs on what we thought was Saddam's head and he seems to have escaped, but no demon ever escapes the power of the blood of the Lamb when a praying saint touches Heaven.

The reason for this is that we cannot defeat the terrorists; we have to defeat the spiritual forces behind them. As Paul said:

For we do not wrestle against flesh and blood, but against principalities, against powers, against the rulers of the darkness of this age, against spiritual hosts of wickedness in the heavenly places.

Ephesians 6:12

Are demon spirits behind orchestrating the terrorist threat? Yes, of course. Where did the demons go that possessed the 19 terrorists on September 11th? What demon is resident in Saddam Hussein? I am not a demon-chaser, but I refuse to believe that those who attacked anyone in such a barbaric way were not demon-possessed. There can be *nothing more important for God's people to do than unite in prayer.* Angels are waiting for assignment and demons are filled with fear that they might be bound; for both know the effectual fervent prayer of a righteous man avails much. (See James 5:16.)

Adonai Oz Leamo Yitein,
The LORD will give strength to His people;
Adonai Yevarech et Amo Bashalom.
The LORD will bless His people with peace.

Psalm 29:11

8

THE ROAD THROUGH BAGHDAD LEADS TO JERUSALEM

"You declare, my friends, that you do not hate the Jews, you are merely anti-Zionist. And I say, let the truth ring forth from the highest mountaintops. Let it echo through the valleys of God's green earth. When people criticize Zionism, they mean Jews. Zionism is nothing less than the dream and ideal of the Jewish people returning to live in their own land."

Martin Luther King[1]

E ven as the war began, all eyes were already turning to its end. At this writing, the siege of Baghdad has begun and Coalition troops seem to be moving in and out of the city at will. If things continue at this pace, hopefully the war in Baghdad will be over by the time you read this book. In any case, Operation Iraqi Freedom will go on for some time, and the Middle East is still far from being peaceful. The battle for Baghdad was never thought to be the end, however, for the road through Baghdad leads to Jerusalem.

And it will always be Jerusalem, not Baghdad, that will determine the balance of power in the Middle East. If Israel, America's only ally in the Middle East, and the only firewall between Islamic terrorism and the West, is weakened any more, then the Islamic genie could easily jump across the sea. Asymmetrical terrorism is the poor man's bomb…a $600 conglomeration of nails, screws, ball bearings, dynamite, a vest, and a few switches.

The End of the Road

The end of the road is coming eventually in Iraq, and once we reach it we'll immediately take out another road map, this one showing the way to a false peace between Israel and the Palestinians. The Quartet—the U.S., U.N., E.U., and Russia—is tuning up to play an anthem of Palestinian statehood as soon as hostilities end. The fact is, they were planning it before the war even began. Some of the members of the Quartet are Secretary of State Colin Powell; Russian Foreign Minister Igor Ivanov; and Mr. Kofi Annan, secretary general of the United Nations. I find it quite troubling of the four power brokers in the Quartet some opposed the U.S. operation in Iraq to fight terrorism, but are delighted to force Israel to accept terrorist organizations as good neighbors.

Whatever domino effect a developing Iraqi democracy may have among other Arab or Muslim countries, the first entity to benefit from the defeat of Saddam Hussein is likely to be the Palestinian Authority. In fact, the two allied leaders, U.S. President George W. Bush and British Prime Minister Tony Blair, agreed even before the outbreak of hostilities on the link between the war on Iraq and the Israeli-Palestinian conflict. Indeed, the entire European political establishment has linked the defeat of Saddam Hussein to a renewed peace process between Israel and the Palestinians. In a statement before the war began, Blair said, "It is precisely now, when we do have all this focus on the issue of weapons of mass destruction and Saddam Hussein and all the things that he has done, that we say to the Arab and Muslim world: 'We accept the obligation of even-handedness, we accept that it is right now that we have to say to people that the issue of peace between Palestinians and Israelis is as important as any other issue to us.'"[2]

President Bush echoed this sentiment after their summit at Camp David: "History requires more of our Coalition than a defeat of a terrible danger. I see an opportunity, as does Prime Minister Blair, to bring renewed hope and progress to the entire

Middle East. Last June 24th, I outlined a vision of two states, Israel and Palestine, living side-by-side in peace and security. Soon, we'll release the Road Map that is designed to help turn that vision into reality. And both America and Great Britain are strongly committed to implementing that Road Map."[3]

Blair responded by noting a date for the public debut of the Road Map: "We both share a complete determination to move this forward. It is, indeed, often overlooked that President Bush is the first U.S. President publicly to commit himself to a two-state solution: an Israel confident of its security and a viable Palestinian state. And I welcome the decision announced recently to publish the road map as soon as the confirmation of the new Palestinian prime minister is properly administered."[4]

But President Bush is going to have to make some difficult choices as the war comes to a close. I know from a first-hand, personal interview with him that Bush is a man of faith who believes the Bible, whereas others who help determine U.S. foreign policy have bought into the "O" word, as in "occupied territories." He is surrounded with bright minds indeed, but regretfully some that do not see Jerusalem any more important than Johannesburg, nor Israel more significant than Istanbul.

Bush has confronted Saddam, the godfather of Islamic state-sponsored terrorism, declaring, "It's time to show your cards." Whereas, the State Department is eager to reshuffle the deck in order to quell the anger throughout the Arab world over the war in Iraq. Powell and others in the U.S. would be very proud to have a part in developing a Palestinian state within Israel's current borders. There are only a couple small problems with this: The God of the Bible, the Bible itself, and

> *Bush confronted Saddam, the godfather of Islamic state-sponsored terrorism, declaring, "It's time to show your cards."*

52 million Bible-believing Americans. It would be a terrible mistake for President Bush to legitimize the P.L.O., and weaken Israel for appeasement. This in no way will strengthen our hand, but will instead send a signal that crime does indeed pay. Therefore we need to pray for President Bush, that he will oppose the road map.

The State Department's "Road Map" plan partners us with the U.N., the E.U., and Russia—none of which supported the war on Iraq. Once Saddam gets walloped, Powell plans to "make friends again" with these entities by bartering Israel's land, buying into the Arab myth that Jewish housing construction in the disputed territories—namely the West Bank, the Gaza Strip, and the Golan Heights—is the root of all the problems in the Middle East. It seems that the State Department owes neither Syria, Iran, nor Libya an apology for putting them on the "state-sponsor of terrorism" list. Secretary Powell will just wave the wand of "Palestinian statehood" and everyone will be happy again.

Arafat challenged me at the U.N. in Geneva in 1988, saying, "Bethlehem is the Muslim town where the first Palestinian, Jesus, was born,"[5] when I had the boldness to tell him at his press conference that Jesus was Jewish and from the Jewish town of Bethlehem. Islam had not even come into being in New Testament days, nor was the "O" word used to refer to Jews at that time, but rather to the Romans. I have to admit, I don't think he appreciated my comments very much! As I quoted from the Bible, Arafat screamed, "Shut up! Shut up! What must I do to make you shut up, striptease for you? That would be absurd!"

And Bethlehem is just one of the issues on the dividing line. What about Jericho? What about Jerusalem?

How will Bush reconcile his faith in the Bible, where Christianity was born in east Jerusalem, with a Road Map that calls it "O" land? When Jesus predicted that, after His death and resurrection, He would return, the time would be after an undivided Jerusalem was back in Jewish hands. It seems now that the ownership of Jerusalem is coming down to the Quartet and politics, and not the prophets and prophecy. However, God still has the deciding vote!

Israel's Right to Exist

Looking back to Genesis 12:3 we read God's words to
Abraham: *"I will bless those who bless you, And I will curse him who
curses you."* Fortunately, the United States has been a great friend
of the reborn Jewish State of Israel during its history. America
was the first country to grant official recognition to the emerging
country in 1948 on the direct orders of President Harry Truman.
The Russians also rushed into the U.N. to recognize tiny Israel in
1948, but they thought they could turn it into one of their satellite
states. They had not read the Bible. Truman could not let that
happen and had to recognize Israel first.

However, there has always been an undercurrent of opposition
to Israel in America. This was evident early on when the State
Department warned President Truman that he would incur the
wrath of oil-rich Arab nations if he supported Israel in the crucial
United Nation's statehood vote. Even though the State
Department released a Top Security telegraph minutes before that
the U.S. was going to recognize a Jewish State, Harry Truman
crossed out the words "Jewish State" when he signed the United
States recognition document and wrote in "State of Israel"
instead. If you would like a free copy of both of these, write me. I
would be delighted to send them to you.

The policy fight, and the underlying spiritual struggle behind it,
continues to this very day. With an eye on the flow of Arab oil
supplies and wealth, many major corporations and one-world
globalists are especially critical of Israel. They are deeply disturbed by the ongoing Arab-Israeli conflict and would do almost
anything to see it resolved. In fact, most would be content with
Hitler's solution — the destruction of the "troublesome" Jewish
people. Today that extends to the elimination of the Jewish State.

The United States is still Israel's closest ally among the nations.
However, many of our actions have contributed to undermining
Israel's viability and thus her chances to survive in the hostile

Muslim Middle East. My contention that America has a mixed record concerning Israel may surprise some readers.

But the facts are clear. Various U.S. administrations have been the main movers and shakers in the so-called "land for peace" process, in which Israel is asked to abandon strategic territory in exchange for mere promises of peace from surrounding Arab enemies.

Since its establishment in 1948, the State of Israel has sought peace with its neighbors through direct negotiations. However, its efforts have not been met with similar cooperation from surrounding Arab countries. Since Israel's birth, Arab nations have wanted a united front against "the Zionist entity." All have rejected Israel's right to exist and have, in fact, adopted 35 resolutions in the U.N. effectively calling for the dismantling of a Zionist.

An exception to this occurred in the 1970s when Egypt accepted Israel's offer to negotiate face-to-face. The late Egyptian leader Anwar Sadat joined in bilateral negotiations leading to the 1978 Camp David peace treaty. Since then peace has prevailed along the two countries' mutual borders. A praying prime minister by the name of Menachem Begin got his prayer answered. I remember a day in his office studying the Bible together as he looked for scriptures to justify his decision. He really wanted God's blessing on his nation. He was a man with a deep faith.

The Fallacy of "Land for Peace"

In a nutshell, the whole "land for peace" issue can be summed up as follows: The P.L.O. wants to control Judea and Samaria and the Gaza Strip and wants East Jerusalem as their capital.

The sticking point for the Jews is that God gave them that land and forbade them to sell it.

The land shall not be sold permanently, for the land is Mine; for you are strangers and sojourners with Me.

Leviticus 25:23

It is no secret that even supposed friends of Israel, including the United States and some of the president's advisors, have adopted a kind of "end-justifies-the-means theology" to explain away the Jews' rightful claim to the land that God promised them. They want to "replace" such troublesome passages of scripture with more convenient and politically correct beliefs. Implementing such actions contrary to the directions of Scripture is treading on very thin ice.

The Bottom Line!

The goal of the Road Map is the creation of "A Two-State Solution to the Palestinian/Israeli Conflict," in other words, The Palestinian Authority would get land within the present borders of Israel within which they would set up the government of Palestine. This state would be independent and sovereign, including "maximum contiguous territory," meaning that they would share borders with no protective "buffer zones" between them. The Quartet Road Map is not an Israeli invention nor is it something Israel is likely to embrace eagerly. Some reasons for this are that the Road Map rejects Israel's control of its borders, requires arms limitations, requires Israel to surrender control of air space, etc. following official elections in the Palestine Authority of its prime minister along with his appointment of a cabinet.

Another of the first goals is to have an international conference (like Madrid after the 1991 Gulf War) for the purpose of "initiating negotiations leading to declaration of a Palestine State with temporary borders." The second conference would be in 2004 to initiate negotiations for a permanent agreement.

The Quartet is the instrument by which a sovereign Palestine state will take form. The Quartet will have supreme oversight and decision-making control. This outline again calls for the total withdrawal of Israel to the 1967 pre-Six Day War borders. (A proposal initiated by the Saudi Arabians.) The guidelines for this would be as follows:

1. Jerusalem/Israel must agree to reopen all Palestine offices and institutions dealing with commerce, business, and economy, which were closed in East Jerusalem, including, of course, the Orient House. The bottom line is that the Palestine Authority would be entering into negotiations on an equal footing with Israel and the Quartet concerning the "permanent agreement" to draw the borders for Jerusalem, refugee areas, and settlements.

2. Israel must accept the "O" (Occupied) word and freeze all settlement activity, which threaten contiguously populated Palestine regions, including areas around Jerusalem.

3. Concerning the declaration of a Palestinian State with temporary borders, Israel must allow maximum geographic contiguity, including further measures concerning uprooting settlements that interrupt territorial continuity. The Road Map demands an international conference to attain peace on all fronts, including the Syrian-Lebanese disputes with Israel.

4. The Quartet will guarantee that all sides implement all obligations simultaneously. This totally contradicts Israel's desires that only after full implementation by the Palestinians will Israel implement their part. For example, the Palestine's obligation to eradicate terror will be equivalent to Israeli obligations concerning settlements activity.

5. The Quartet will initiate an International Observer Force. Israel is not asking for an International Observer Force, and certainly not from the U.N., E.U., and Russia. Such "observers" would have to be supportive of Israeli rights, to say the least.

6. The Quartet, not Israel, will decide when to recognize the Palestinian State. Again "maximum contiguous territory" meaning Israel would have to release control of borders, arms limitations, control of airspace, and more. The Quartet, not Israel, will determine when conditions are ripe for progress.

7. The Road Map also totally ignores Israeli demands such as cessation of terror, collection of illegal armaments, and cessation of incitement—in other words Israel's decision-making control is severely restricted.[6]

How will the Quartet attempt to force Israel to accept this Road Map? Plain and simple—economic blackmail.

Israel's Gross National Product (GNP) for 2002 was $100 billion. Israel needs a GNP of $100 billion to balance its budget at its present rate of growth. It lost more than $15 billion in 2003 because of terrorism (this figure is derived from its defense budget and lost income). Its total exports for 2002 were $28 billion. During Operation Iraqi Freedom, the U.S. promised to satisfy Israel's request for the $9 billion in U.S. loan guarantees and another $1 billion in aid, which amounts to over 10 percent of Israel's needed GNP. At the time of this writing, Israel still has not received the promised funds even though they are told, "The check is on the way."

The Quartet simply has to say, in a whisper, "Obey the Golden Rule: we have the gold; we will make the rules and you will follow them. If you don't, then, sorry, we cannot allow your exports into our countries. You see, we have tariff and trade issues to deal with. It has nothing to do with blackmail."

Russia not only possesses economic leverage (Israel made $169.2 million from Russia in 2001 [last available figure]), but they have an even greater lever—Russian Jews that want to go home! Up until 1989, Russian Jews were not able to leave, but since then one million have come to Israel. There is another one million who are experiencing anti-Semitism. With one simple word their visa application would be rejected if they tried to get out.

Israel will be forced to follow their rules or become a bankrupt nation. We're talking about more than a third of Israel's entire GNP lost.

The Bible predicts a day when the Antichrist will do something similar:

> *And through his policy also he shall cause craft* [trade] *to prosper in his hand; and he shall magnify himself in his heart, and by peace shall destroy many, he shall stand up against the Prince of Princes; but he shall be broken without hand.*
>
> Daniel 8:25 KJV [author's insert]

The Quartet's Makeover of the P.L.O.

As President Bush has been quite open about refusing to accept Yasser Arafat as the representative of the new Palestinian

Authority as outlined in the Road Map, the P.L.O. was forced to find someone else to be the PA's Prime Minister. They didn't look far. Since they couldn't select Arafat, they selected his longtime deputy and cofounder of Fatah, Mahmoud Abbas (who is also known as Abu Mazen).

As you may remember from the Preface, Abbas was crucial in the P.L.O.'s rejection of Israel's comprehensive peace plan at Camp David in 2000 and also coordinated the P.L.O.'s. negotiating team during the 1991 Madrid Conference. He has been labeled a "moderate" by the Quartet, even though he claims that the Nazis killed "only a few hundred thousand Jews,"[7] not millions during the Second World War—comments he was later forced to retract for political reasons.

The majority of Abbas' new cabinet members are also from Fatah. Though he has yet to be labeled a puppet of Arafat, it is unclear what his role will be as Arafat will still be directing all of the Palestinian Authority's foreign affairs, including the PA's negotiations with Israel. One has to wonder, as a prime minister without a country to run, what other responsibilities can exist besides foreign affairs?

This sham might actually be comical, if it didn't appear that the U.S. and the Quartet were buying into it. President Bush's own comments at the recent third Operation Iraqi Freedom summit with Prime Minister Tony Blair in Northern Ireland indicate that he totally accepts Abbas' appointment as if Abbas had nothing to do with Arafat and the other Fatah terrorists: "I'm pleased with the new leader of the Palestinian Authority. I look forward to him finally putting his cabinet in place so we can release the Road Map."[8] He also said that he was confident that "substantive progress" could be made on peace now that Abbas was in place.

Soon after that, on Friday April 11, 2003, British Foreign Secretary Jack Straw told Palestinian Authority Chairman Yasser Arafat that the International Road Map for Peace would be released in the next few days. Israel Radio reported the next day, Saturday the 12th, that Straw had also told Arafat that the international Road Map for peace would be released in the next few days. Straw also told Arafat that the international community was fully committed to the implementation of the Road Map.

Nabil Abu Rudeineh, a top aid to Arafat, reported that Straw told Arafat "all the international community is committed to help implement the Road Map Peace plan. European diplomats announced the plan would be presented for implementation without any changes in its text as soon as Mahmoud Abbas approves the new Palestinian cabinet.

Israel's Response

Israel does not support the Quartet Plan in that it does not explicitly condition statehood on an end to terrorism. Former Secretary of State James Baker called President Bush to urge him to "keep his father's tradition" and take advantage of the "window of opportunity" presented by the Road Map. That same weekend, April 12-13, 2003, Mr. Baker also said in a meeting in Toronto that the U.S. must "pressure Israel aggressively" to ensure peace in the region.

Dov Weisglass, Prime Minister Sharon's chief of Staff, immediately flew to Washington to attempt to do damage control. The Israeli Diplomat presented a list of 15 points of contention to the Road Map plan, which include the following:

- Any step forward made in the plan must be made as a result of actions, rather than a set timetable;
- a settlement freeze will only take place after a prolonged period of security quiet;
- the Saudi Arabian peace proposal will not be considered as a starting place for negotiations;
- a Palestinian state can be established, with temporary borders, only after the destruction of the terror infrastructure in the territories; and only with Israel's agreement; and
- the U.S. will oversee the implementation and not the Quartet.

The U.S. response was that the Road Map would continue forward with no changes.

This same response was echoed on April 17, 2003, during the EU Summit in Athens, Greece. United Nations Secretary General Kofi Annan and Russian Foreign Minister Igor Ivanov called for the immediate publication of the Road Map as soon as the Palestinian prime minister elect, Abu Mazen, had set up his cabinet. "We expect that after the Road Map has been formally released, we will receive the additional comments from the Israeli side, and we expect to receive comments from the prime minister of the Palestine Authority," Secretary of State Colin Powell told reporters. The confusing part of it all is what does "formal release" really mean? The parties both have the Road Map, and Powell has already told Israel following appeals by them there will be no changes in it.

However, the Terrorists Remain Undeterred

The strangest part of this entire theater of the absurd and festival of hypocrisy is that while the U.S. State Department has been moving forward all through the war with their plan, so has the P.L.O. Fuad Abu Hijleh, a Palestinian political analyst, said it this way:

"The Arabs had one case, that of Palestine, and one occupation, the Israeli occupation. However, this morning the Arabs woke up to a new case and new occupation. Now we have a second Palestine in Iraq."

Meanwhile, on the same day, the leader of the Syrian-backed Islamic Jihad organization in the Gaza Strip, Abdallah al-Shami, described the collapse of Saddam's regime as an "earthquake." He said the end of the war in Iraq would only increase his group's determination to continue terrorist attacks against Israel.

Islamic Jihad was also one of two Palestinian groups that recruited volunteers to fight against the American and British forces in Iraq. The other group was Palestinian Authority Chairman Yasser Arafat's Fatah, which sent hundreds from Lebanon and Syria on suicide missions against the U.S. and British soldiers during the war. There were also hundreds of Palestinians waving posters of

Saddam and Iraqi flags in marching in the West Bank and Gaza Strip to protest against the U.S.-led invasion of Iraq.

The Hamas terrorists also vowed to step up attacks on Israel, and urged Iraqis to carry out suicide bombings against invading U.S. and British forces. Senior Hamas leader Abdel Aziz Rantisi told Reuters in the Gaza Strip:

> "Iraqis should prepare explosive belts and would-be martyrs [suicide bombers] to combat the U.S. occupiers.
> "The American aggressors, the American invaders are now on Iraqi soil; therefore, Iraqis must confront them with all possible means, including martyrdom [suicide] operations."

Nor were Iraq's other Muslim neighbors silent. Syria also encouraged Palestinian refugees in Lebanon to volunteer to fight against Coalition forces in Iraq, and even provided buses to take them from Damascus to Baghdad. Lebanese sources estimated that hundreds of these volunteers made the journey, though not all without incident. One busload of these Syrian-sponsored volunteers was hit by a U.S. missile some 50 kilometers inside Iraqi territory, killing five and wounding dozens. At the time, the missile strike was described as an accident of war. Now that the Palestinian volunteer connection has become known, however, there is speculation that the missile was fired intentionally, perhaps as a warning to discourage other volunteers. Syria was the only country bordering Iraq during the war that kept its border crossings open.

Syrian military analyst Hitham al-Kilani said in an interview on al-Jazeera on March 24 that, "The Syrian border was opened to Syrian, Arab, and Muslim volunteers wishing to reach Iraq and participate in the fighting against the American invasion." Kilani also said the Syrian border is also open to Iraqi refugees seeking to enter Syria.

Around the same time, *Ha'aretz Daily* newspaper reported that in the months prior to the war, Syria had been purchasing military equipment on behalf of the Iraqi Army and delivering it on trucks from the Syrian port of Latakia to Iraq. The material, bought from

East European countries, included engines for Iraq's Russian-made tanks and aircraft, as well as tank carriers from Germany.

On April 13th, White House officials said Huda Salih Mahdi Ammash, nicknamed "Chemical Sally," and Rihab Taha, "Dr. Germ," both experts in Iraq's biological-weapons program, are in Syria.

Another report by *The Jerusalem Post* stated that American and British forces were attacked by Palestinians and Jordanians who had come to Iraq to fight the Coalition forces. "They executed an integrated attack," said a U.S. Army's 2nd Brigade's operations officer over the radio. "They utilized snipers and accurate artillery as well as suicide bombers and RPGs." The information on the identity of the forces was gleaned from prisoners of war caught during the fighting. It was reported later that the defense of Baghdad was largely being carried out by some 5,000 Palestinian, Syrian, and Jordanian troops. The Republican Guard's units were already largely eroded down to 25 percent of their original numbers.

Later it was revealed that Iraqis surrendering to U.S. forces had detonated Palestinian-style explosive belts strapped to their bodies as the Americans approached them. Subsequently, all surrendering forces were ordered to undress before approaching U.S. forces to prevent a recurrence of such incidents.

America's Approaching Turning Point

Despite these actions, further evidence that the U.S. government is already taking steps to support this Road Map is apparent by the fact that the United States is still withholding its nine billion in loan guarantees and one billion in aid from Israel at this writing (April 2003). (A similar $10 billion carrot and stick game was played in 1991 forcing Israel to the Madrid Peace Conference so that they could force Israel into a land giveaway.) The financial assistance was being denied until a new government was formed following the Israeli elections on January 28, 2003, and was even denied when the Iraqi war began. It was being held up to push Israel "to take a brave gamble for peace" such as those outlined in the Road Map.

At that time, the State of Israel voted in favor of the Likud government that opposes a Palestinian state. Former Prime Minister Benjamin Netanyahu (now Minister of Finance); Ehud Olmert, the former mayor of Jerusalem (now Vice Premier); and Natan Sharansky, a cabinet minister who speaks for Israel's one million Russian Jews, strongly oppose a P.L.O. state. Many believe the withholding of this economic assistance was an attempt to force Prime Minister Ariel Sharon to reject a Likud government and form a coalition government with the Labor Party.

The Labor Party consists mainly of liberals who do not believe the Bible and who will accept a Palestinian state. (This was the same party that was willing to accept the plan presented by former President Bill Clinton to divide Jerusalem, another instance of replacement theology.) This party has now accepted the Quartet's plan that calls for a Palestinian state and for Israel to withdraw to her pre-1967 borders within three years. Shimon Peres of the Israel Labor Party has said, "We approve the role of the Quartet."[9] This would again mean the division of Jerusalem.

Russia, the European Union, China, the United Nations, and the Arab world have all expressed their support of this Road Map plan, but it is really up to the United States to spearhead it and convince Israel of its validity.

According to sources in Jerusalem, tiny Israel accepts the Road Map in principle, but has a number of reservations—about 15. It is difficult for Israel not to accept the Road Map in principle when $10 billion is at stake, along with incurring the rage of literally the entire world. This is because, if there is one thing Israel has learned following its post-Oslo afflictions, it is that it cannot afford to make unilateral concessions. If there is going to be something really new in the post-Saddam "New Middle East," it will be a return to traditional Middle Eastern bargaining: An Israeli quid for a Palestinian quo.

The New Middle East will not evolve in response to a Security Council resolution or a public relations campaign by the European Community. It is not the proverbial diplomatic omelet that can be created only by breaking eggs. The eggs must indeed

> ## The only Road Map for peace is the Bible.

be broken—but, as at the beginning of new life, from the inside.

The only Road Map for peace is the Bible. Years ago in the White House, the then-National Security Advisor told me that the status of Jerusalem must be determined by negotiations. I responded, "God does not recognize your non-recognition. He will not negotiate with you or anyone."

On his kibbutz before he died, Israel's first prime minister, David Ben-Gurion, told me that the British once told him, "The British Mandate will be your Bible." He responded, "The Bible will be my mandate."

I also remember discussing scripture and praying with Prime Minister Yitzhak Rabin in his office in 1993—and then attending his state funeral after his "brave gamble for peace" backfired and cost him his life. As I stood and watched at the graveside of this great man of Israel, a bead of sweat rolled down Bill Clinton's face. It was nothing massive, nothing noticeable. In fact, if you weren't watching closely, you would never have seen it, but there it was, glistening in the afternoon sun—a tiny bead running down the forehead of the most powerful man in the world. Neither was the face the same as the popular pictures of it. The carefully practiced expressions weren't there. Instead, the president's face looked sunken, tired.

I looked across and as Edward Kennedy tossed bits of dirt from the graves of his brothers, John and Robert, his hand trembled. This man, Massachusetts' powerful liberal senator with the family name of American royalty, looked shaken.

Former U.S. President George H. W. Bush stood there—the man who had fearlessly fought the Gulf War in 1991—looking pale. Former President Jimmy Carter looked older and frailer that he ever has before.

Forty-four U.S. Congressmen stood in the vicinity, all looking shaken. Eighty-six world leaders from all over the globe stood by gloomily, each showing something on their faces that the television cameras never see, the news photographers never seem to capture, and the newspapers never write about.

As I watched the funeral of fallen Israeli Prime Minister Yitzhak Rabin, the most powerful people in the world stood around in unison, looking helpless.

Around the graveside stood people who had withstood coup attempts, had bravely stood against public opinion, had survived ruthless media assaults, had looked dead into the eye of nuclear war and had not flinched. Some of these men and women literally have their finger on the button that could touch off global nuclear war and devastation of unprecedented proportions and beyond the imaginations of even the most horrific fiction writers.

The gathered dignitaries controlled economies that measure in the trillions of dollars every single day. Every day they deal with pressures most other people on the planet can only have breathless nightmares about.

Literally at the snap of their fingers, the gathered world leaders can command millions of soldiers into battle—they could embroil the entire world into war in a matter of hours. They have faced down scandals, assassination attempts, terrorist attacks, and natural disasters. But as I scanned the powerful men and women staring impotently down into the grave of Yitzhak Rabin, I saw corners of mouths trembling, eyes twitching, sweat rolling, and hands shaking.

I have been to dozens of funerals over the years in Israel as Jews have died taking the brave gamble for peace. I know why the shortest scripture in the New Testament is "Jesus wept." He must be weeping now. Consider this: If America had simply recognized Jerusalem as Israel's capital and its borders after after the Arab world prepared to attack in 1967, then the Arabs in Israel would be living better than any Arab in the Middle East. There never would have been a Palestinian state that was an invention to accommodate an Egyptian terrorist by the name of Arafat who could not find a way to establish a military base to conduct terrorism in Israel. He was kicked out of Jordan, Syria, and Lebanon, because he only knew how to destroy countries and not build them.

We need to believe the Bible—all of it—simple as that—which includes the story of the Promised Land and the Ten Commandments—especially the one that says, *"Thou shalt not kill."*

Politics or Prophecy?

Can the United States have any other mandate and succeed? The U.S. needs to be very careful how it walks down this road—there are a lot of sharp corners and going over the edge of them could lead to deadly and explosive circumstances, if not for us, definitely for Israel. As God told Abraham:

"I will bless those who bless you,
And I will curse him who curses you;
And in you all the families of the earth shall be blessed."

Genesis 12:3

> *We need to pray for wisdom in our government and protection for peace in the city of Jerusalem.*

We can ill afford to turn our back on Abraham and his descendants.

Can we as Americans maintain our faith and not support and protect Israel in this process? My response would definitely be "No!" We need to let our President know that compromising Israel's safety and existence in this process is not acceptable; then we need to pray for wisdom in our government and protection for peace in the city of Jerusalem. The bottom line is man proposes but God disposes. If America loses the blessing of God, then the war on terrorism will be lost no matter how hard we try.

"And let us not trust to human effort alone, but humbly acknowledge the power and goodness of Almighty God, who presides over the destiny of nations, and who has at times been revealed in our county's history; let us invoke His aid and His blessing upon our labors."

Grover Cleveland

9

WHAT LIES AHEAD FOR THE U.S.?

"Those who cannot remember the past are condemned to repeat it."

George Santayana[1]
Life of Reason, Reason in Common Sense

In October of 1991, a Middle East Peace Conference was convened at the Royal Palace in Madrid, Spain. I spoke up at the conclusion of then-Secretary of State James Baker's remarks. I asked, "Why can't America recognize Jerusalem as Israel's capital?" Baker was angered by my remarks and said he refused to be entangled in a fruitless debate: The status of Jerusalem should be determined by negotiations.

To this day, America has refused to recognize Jerusalem as Israel's capital.[2] This is a grave mistake. I have shouted this warning from the White House in Washington to the Royal Palace in Madrid as I cried out to the world leaders with the words, "God does not recognize your non-recognition position!"

Later at that same conference, I stood in shocked silence as I looked into the eyes of President George H. W. Bush. Israel had not been allowed to join the Coalition forces of the 1991 Gulf War, because all the anti-Semitic Arab countries were screaming against them. Our President also asked Israel not to retaliate when they were bombarded with 39 Scud missiles attacks, and they honored his request. For their cooperation in this, we rewarded them by freezing a $10 billion dollar loan guarantee that Israel needed to provide housing for refugees, mostly Russian Jews. Israel's enemies were appeased again when Israel was forced to agree to give up land for peace—peace that has never come. Historically the U.S. has been Israel's closest ally, but the lure of OPEC oil has been chipping away at America's dedication to that alliance.

The U.S. gave Syria one billion dollars which Syria turned around and used to purchase North Korean missiles. Many of those missiles are in Lebanon in the hands of the Palestinian terrorist organization Hizbullah and are aimed at the cities of Israel.[3]

As a nation, we are treading on extremely thin ice. A turn against Israel is a turn against the apple of God's eye.

> *For he who touches you [Zion] touches the apple of His eye. For surely I will shake My hand against them, and they shall become spoil for their servants.*
> Zechariah 2:8-9 [author's insert]

America is caught in the crosshairs of our own crossroads—if we change our historic stance and turn against Israel, we pull the trigger. God forbid that we should be the ones to start the war between Babylon (the Iraq of Revelation) and Jerusalem that will ultimately end at the end of the age, and then side with Babylon for the final battle.

We Must Look Back to See Forward

The world really has not changed since the attacks of September 11th, it is just that America has finally entered into a world it before quietly denied existed. From past activities, Israel knew that one day something like those attacks would happen and even tried to warn us, but we thought we knew better. It is time that we opened our eyes to the truth.

Operation Iraqi Freedom will not end with victory in Baghdad. It will take years to stabilize Iraq. And that will not happen without mighty prayer; otherwise, we will wake up to another Lebanon in time. What is our best course of action through the times ahead? Perhaps the best key to the future is the events of the Middle East's recent past.

Operation Iraqi Freedom will not end with victory in Baghdad.

First of all, as the Iraqi war ends and things begin to settle down, Muslim terrorists will lay the same explosive groundwork for civil war in Iraq that they laid in Lebanon in the 1970s. Underground cell groups will be formed, munitions stockpiled, and suicide bombers armed with whatever they can get their hands on—conventional explosives or weapons of mass destruction—will strike at whatever foreign soldiers who are there to keep the peace, but especially at Americans.

If My people who are called by My name will humble themselves, and pray and seek My face, and turn from their wicked ways, then I will hear from Heaven, and will forgive their sin and heal their land.

2 Chronicles 7:14

A free, democratic Iraq is a critical threat to the "family-run corporation" structure of most of the Middle East's Islamic governments. Power to the people is the enemy of any dictatorship and unless the people are suppressed, they will not be able to be controlled. Just as the people of Basra cheered British troops as their tanks rolled into the city marking the elimination of Saddam's influence there, Islamic dictatorships know that their rule can only be maintained by the bullet, not the ballot. As I said earlier, Islamic governments fear America's most dangerous weapon, the economic stealth bomber that inspires democracy. That weapon collapsed the former U.S.S.R. and Eastern Europe. They know that drastic times require drastic measures to save their dictatorships. They will give the subtle head-nod to their Islamic fundamentalist clerics.

The Battle for Hearts and Minds

America's first pillar of its republic in the Bill of Rights promises the freedom of religion. In the years since that structure was established, Americans have slowly acquiesced to the idea that, in our great American melting pot, it is enough to believe something and that all beliefs and structures of worship are "good." In other words, it is better to have some set of moral standards than none at all. But we need to wake up to the fact that not all religions are good—some just poise their adherents to kill.

For this reason America has to undertake an incredible reeducation program, which, by its own statutes, it can't. The freedom of religion in the Constitution is more like freedom from religion in today's interpretations of that freedom. The U.S. government has nothing to offer that can replace the hatred and change the hearts that Wahabism has bred. Secularism is a better answer than terrorism in a political sense, but the consequences are just as dire in a spiritual sense. To impose a secular democracy the U.S. will have to dethrone an Islam theocracy.

> *We may be able to liberate their lands, but we cannot liberate their hearts — only God can do that.*

The only alternative is for praying saints to take the new front lines. What we may well be seeing in America's victory in Iraq is the same opportunity we saw at the fall of the U.S.S.R. We must understand that no battles are won in the physical realm until they are won in the spiritual realm — through prayer — and every battle that is not won in the spiritual realm — through prayer — is lost in the physical realm.

We may be able to liberate their lands, but we cannot liberate their hearts — only God can do that.

The Fall of Hussein Is Not the Fall of Terrorism

Iraq is not the only state that supported terrorism, though it may well have been one of the most open about it. If God-fearing, praying people sleep, the dry wood of terrorism will ignite as the rage of Islamic fundamentalism boils over afresh and could spread into a Third World War.

That the war on terrorism could turn into a "holy war" between the East and the West, I don't doubt, but I am not convinced it needs to either. The prophecies in the Bible will happen, make no mistake about that, and our prayers will not change that, but they will affect how smoothly we approach that time and it will also affect how smoothly we make it through. This is not Armageddon's season, nor was September 11th to be—but regretfully praying Christians in America were asleep at the post when the warn alarms were going off before September 11th.

The words of Alfred Lord Tennyson are as true today as they were the day they were spoken: "More things are wrought by prayer than this world dreams of."

This book is a call to action. The words of Sir Winston Churchill are ringing in my ears. "Never give in, never, never, never, never— in nothing, great or small, large or petty—never give in except to conviction of honor and good sense." Terrorist attacks can shake the foundations of our biggest building, but they cannot shake the foundation of a praying, God-fearing American no matter how frail. Their acts may shatter steel, but they cannot dent the steel in the heart of even a praying child who refuses to compromise. There are kingdoms of darkness that must be overthrown; there are lions of terror whose mouths must be shut; there are flames of fear that need to be quenched; and they can! This book is an appeal to those with moral conviction to stand up, speak up, and pray up.

I stated at the beginning of this book that on the walls of the CIA building in Virginia are the words, *"And ye shall know the Truth and the Truth shall set you free."* My prayer is that God will engrave these words on the walls of our hearts as well.

Let me make this point before I go on. Many seem to take the stance that since the Bible foretells us that the end is coming, they might as well throw up their hands and let it come. This is not the right answer and totally misses the heart of God. As individuals have the decision whether or not to follow God, so do nations. We may definitely be heading towards Armageddon, but what will happen next is not Armageddon—that is a long way down the road in prophecy. Without prayer the real battle against terrorism cannot be won. That battle will not end with Iraq, it will continue. There is no question the horror that could have happened in Iraq did not. It wasn't because of pure military genius, but indeed because of the power of prayer. A battle was truly fought and won in the heavenlies. That battle must be waged again for the safety of troops in harm's way and for Israel. The war has not ended, it has just begun. We need to pray ourselves and our nations through these perilous times. As Jesus advised us:

> *"When you hear of wars and commotions, do not be terrified; for these things must come to pass first, but the end will not come immediately....*
> *"But take heed to yourselves, lest your hearts be weighed down with carousing, drunkenness, and cares of this life, and that Day come on you unexpectedly. For it will come as a snare on all those who dwell on the face of the whole earth. Watch therefore, and pray always that you may be counted worthy to escape all these things that will come to pass, and to stand before the Son of Man."*
>
> Luke 21:9, 34-36

With this in mind, I want to note that I don't think we necessarily will have to go into open warfare with all of these nations. We still have a major trump card we can play, and control of Iraq gives us another ace. We can play the same hand that toppled the U.S.S.R. — economic pressure. The U.S.S.R. and Eastern Europe fell as the stealthy economic lever was pulled, and the "evil empire" collapsed like a house of cards.

Proverbs 13:22 says, *"The wealth of the sinner is stored up for the righteous."* Under Iraqi soil lies more than 112 billion barrels of oil — the world's second largest reserve behind Saudi Arabia. It is actually sitting atop the largest oil deposit in the world — roughly 60 percent of the earth's total petroleum reserves — with Iran, Kuwait, and Saudi Arabia. It also holds more than 110 trillion cubic feet of gas (according to the U.S. Energy Information Administration). U.S. control of this oil could break the oil cartel and drop the price of oil from thirty dollars per barrel to ten dollars per barrel. This would bring oil-rich, pro-terrorist Muslim countries to their knees. It could also ignite an economic boom such as the world has never seen. Oil-rich Arab dictatorships that are harboring or supporting terrorists will have two choices: Cooperate with the war on terrorism or go bankrupt.

In addition and despite the threat of terrorism in the region, Iraq is still strategically located to address other terrorist states. Its border with Iran is just one example of this. With a U.S. military command and control center firmly established in Iraq, terrorist states will have panic attacks by the minute. This is why, I believe, every conceivable pressure possible will be attempted to embarrass and humiliate America, especially in 2004, a presidential election year. In a meeting with Isser Harel more than six months before Ronald Reagan was elected president, I asked Harel, "Who do you think will be president...Jimmy Carter or Ronald Reagan?" He smiled and said, "That decision will probably be determined by powers in the Middle East, and not in America."

I looked at him questioningly, not understanding his comment. Harel said, "Mike, if the Islamic fundamentalists who are controlling your embassy in Iran release the hostages, Carter's presidency will most likely be saved, and Reagan will lose. But I have a strong feeling they will not do that.... They think Reagan is an actor, and no threat to them. The word on the street is when Ronald Reagan lifts his hand to be sworn in, they will release the hostages."

There will be a major attempt to pressure the President to pull out of Iraq. He will be advised to offer up Israel to the new world order, giving the P.L.O. their "fair" share of the Bible Land and its crown jewel, Jerusalem. The spin doctors will advise the President, "You have been a war president. Forget Syria and Iran for now. Project yourself. As a peace president, focus on Israel and the Palestinians. Don't forget the fellow who shouted at your father, "It's the economy, stupid." If this happens, America may lose the war on terrorism and President Bush may not be elected to a second term. We need to pray for President Bush—that he realizes that in order for our country to be blessed, we must support Jerusalem—and that he will not give into these pressures to give this land away.

Terrorist cells thrive in secret and need money and state sponsorship to survive. All of that could change with a free, democratic Iraq.

But, there is something to consider, however. A democratic, empowered Germany elected the most insane madman the world had ever seen, Adolph Hitler. If democracy comes to moderate Saudi Arabia, and everyone has a vote, the Wahabi clerics and masses will prevail. Osama bin Laden will become president by a landslide. What will a democracy in Iraq look like? Obviously, if a true democracy becomes a reality, 65 percent of the people who vote are Islamic Shiites. A democracy will give Iraq the ability for Islamic Shiites to control the country.

Since the Islamic revolution in Iran in 1979, hard-line religious leadership has defined Shiite Islam for its 120 million followers worldwide. Iran will do the same in Iraq. For more than 1300 years, Najaf was the center of the Shiite world. The son-in-law of the prophet Muhammad, Ali, who was the founder of the faith is buried there. In his famous mosque is still an important pilgrimage for his followers. Five other imams, all successors of Ali, are buried in other cities in Iraq including his son, Hussein, whose death in battle has evoked the cult of martyrdom among Shiites. Shiite clerics believe they are just as much God's representatives on earth as the Pope, and will use all of their power to prove it.

We need to make sure we haven't just replaced Saddam's regime with something worse, or just laid the groundwork for civil war. A war cannot be partially won; the victor is determined by who wins the last battle. We must see this war through until the end, or the next time we have to fight terrorism it could be much worse.

We Need God's Wisdom for Our Leaders

I am not proposing these possibilities as the solutions—this book is not a word from the Lord about every detail of how we are to proceed in Operation Iraqi Freedom or in our war on terrorism. What it is, though, is a call to turn back to God, repent, and pray. Without God's guidance, I sense disaster for our country and our world. On my part, I am not willing to let that happen, thus my passion for writing this book and starting the Jerusalem Prayer Team ministry.

We have so many promises in the Bible of what will happen if God's people turn to Him in prayer that I don't have space in this book to quote them all. All you need to do is open your Bible and you will find them. But I will leave you with this one:

If any of you lacks wisdom, let him ask of God, who gives to all liberally and without reproach, and it will be given to him.

James 1:5

In these times we need God's wisdom more than ever. It is time we get on our knees and faces and go after it.

10

THE WAKE-UP CALL FROM HEAVEN: PREPARING FOR OUR LORD'S COMING!

"So you also, when you see these things happening, know that the kingdom of God is near.... Watch therefore, and pray always that you may be counted worthy to escape all these things that will come to pass, and to stand before the Son of Man."

Luke 21:31,36

Can the war on terrorism be won while God's people sleep? No! A thousand times NO! September 11th was planned, fought, and won before it ever happened. God-fearing Americans were asleep at their posts while demons were working diligently. On September 12, we arose, shook ourselves, and began to cry out to God. But we soon fell asleep again within weeks.

I am sure that the Jews in Jerusalem were just as shocked on March 16th, 587 B.C., when Nebuchadnezzar besieged their capital, and they were dragged off into captivity along with plundered items from the Holy Temple. By the way the 16th was also the day that Bush and Blair announced to the world that there would be war within days if the U.N. could not get Saddam to comply.

There is a war on between light and darkness. The battle did not begin on September 11th. It was planned years before. If the eyes of the Church had been open, perhaps the battle could have been fought and won in prayer before September 11th. The 19 who executed this demonic plan had to have been inspired and directed for a long period of time.

I am certain that the terrorist attacks of our day are not the prophetic will of God for this time, but are the will of hell. Prayer is not the *best* answer; it is the *only* answer. It is not the *last* resort; it is the *only* resort.

Many of us casually clicked off the images of our troops on the front lines of Operation Iraqi Freedom each night thinking that they will take care of it, but the fact is that we have a front line of our own to hold and the fighting needs to be on our knees and faces before God. The American military must fight for our freedom, but it is up to God-fearing Americans to fight for our soldiers' lives and that the peace they win will be lasting.

In the Old Testament, the word *watchman* is often used for those called to intercessory prayer for their people. Just as a watchman in a city stands at the gate to warn the people of a coming enemy and to be the first line of defense, so intercessory prayer warriors are the first line of spiritual defense for our nations and communities. What happens when the watchmen don't do their jobs?

> *What happens when the watchmen don't do their jobs?*

> *But if the watchman sees the sword coming and does not blow the trumpet to warn the people and the sword comes and takes the life of one of them, that man will be taken away because of his sin, but I will hold the watchman accountable for his blood.*
>
> Ezekiel 33:6 NIV

Yes, in many ways the blood of those killed in suicide bombings is on our hands, just as the blood of Christians was on Paul's hands. So what did Paul do about it? What did he say?

> *Therefore I testify to you this day that I am innocent of the blood of all men. For I have not shunned to declare to you the whole counsel of God.*
>
> Acts 20:26-27

Paul declared himself sinless because he turned from his killing ways to saving ways! He repented and followed God. We must turn from apathy to steadfast prayer in the same way! We must get before God and plead our case for the realization of His promises!

Daniel's Example

In the midst of Israel's captivity in Babylonia, God told His people the following through the prophet Jeremiah:

After seventy years are completed at Babylon, I will visit you and perform My good word toward you, and cause you to return to this place. For I know the thoughts that I think toward you, says the LORD, thoughts of peace and not of evil, to give you a future and a hope. Then you will call upon Me and go and pray to Me, and I will listen to you. And you will seek Me and find Me, when you search for Me with all your heart. I will be found by you, says the LORD, and I will bring you back from your captivity; I will gather you from all the nations and from all the places where I have driven you, says the LORD, and I will bring you to the place from which I caused you to be carried away captive.

Jeremiah 29:10-14

God had a plan for their deliverance from before they went into captivity! But the fact of the matter is, over seventy years later, they were still in captivity. What had happened? Did God forget to set His alarm clock and sleep through freeing His people?

No. The answer is, although God had a plan for their rescue and had even given them the timetable for it through Jeremiah, nothing would happen until someone prayed it back to God! God's people needed an Advocate on earth to *ask* for the fulfillment of God's Word. (As James 4:2 says, *"Yet you do not have because you do not ask."*)

In this case, that someone was Daniel:

In the first year of Darius the son of Ahasuerus, of the lineage of the Medes, who was made king over the realm of the Chaldeans—in the first year of his reign I, Daniel, understood by the books the number of the years specified by the word of the LORD through Jeremiah the prophet, that He would accomplish seventy years in the desolations of Jerusalem.
Then I set my face toward the Lord God to make request by prayer and supplications, with fasting, sackcloth, and ashes.

Daniel 9:1-3

After Daniel had read the prophecy in Jeremiah 28:10-14 that the time of the captivity was to last 70 years, he must have done a quick finger count and realized the time was up. Did this make him angry at God for the evil that had been done to them by Babylon? No! Daniel turned to the Lord and repented for the sins of his nation, asked for forgiveness on their behalf, and asked that God's Word and will concerning them would be fulfilled. (See Daniel 9:4-19.) Daniel was told that his prayer had been heard from the moment it was uttered, but the prince of Persia (a demonic being as mentioned in Ephesians 6:12) withstood Gabriel for twenty-one days. He was also told that Michael the archangel had joined Gabriel in battling these demonic powers. (See Daniel 10:10-13.)

And what was the result of Daniel's steadfastness in prayer? Israel was delivered!

Daniel knew that his most important assignment was prayer. That was confirmed to him by the battle in the heavenlies between demons and angels, between good and evil. The city of Babylon was one of the Seven Wonders of the ancient world. It was considered impregnable, but Daniel, through the power of prayer, was able to *"be strong, and carry out great exploits"* (Daniel 11:32). If Daniel could pray and have mighty angels sent to do battle against demon spirits, so can we. Since Daniel lived in the Babylonian Empire, it is quite possible that "the prince of Persia" he fought in the spirit is one of the same spirits we must battle today. But regardless of which spirits are now involved or how many there are, the clarion call is going out to God-fearing people everywhere to man the battle stations and fight the war in prayer.

Just as America has been forced to take the war on terrorism to the battlefields of the nations that sponsor it, we must take our fight to the battlefield in the spiritual realm to defeat the demons that "sponsor" it as well. We must take the battle to the enemy!

Welcoming Back the King!

Pray for the peace of Jerusalem:
"May they prosper who love you.

Peace be within your walls,
Prosperity within your palaces."
For the sake of my brethren and companions,
I will now say, "Peace be within you."
Because of the house of the LORD our God
I will seek your good.

Psalm 122:6-9

When we pray for the peace of Jerusalem we are saying, "Maranatha, come Messiah!"

The Messiah is indeed coming back, and He is coming to Jerusalem. That is something on which both Jews and Christians agree. As Christians, we believe that we know His name, while the Jewish people say they don't. But there is no question that when the Messiah comes, everyone will know His name.

Our Lord was asked by His disciples in Matthew 24:3 KJV, *"What shall be the sign of thy coming, and of the end of the world?"* He clearly gave them the signs beginning with the destruction of the Temple. In verse 2, Jesus prophesied that the Temple would be taken apart stone by stone 40 years before it happened. The fig tree has always been a symbol of the nation of Israel. In verses 32-36, Jesus laid out the key sign of His return, and the end of the age would be the sign of the fig tree. That "fig tree" bloomed on May 14,1948 in fulfillment of Isaiah 66:8: *"Shall the earth be made to bring forth in one day? or shall a nation be born at once?"* Jesus warned to not set dates for "no one would know the day or the hour." The generation that saw the blooming of the fig tree would not pass away until He came.

It was 597 B.C. in the days of Nebuchadnezzar in Babylon that Israel was taken into captivity. Since then, the land of Israel has changed hands 26 times. It has been leveled to the ground five times. But in 1948, the prophecy of Matthew 24 knocked at the door.

A generation is most often defined as 70-80 years. If a person had been 10 years old in 1948 when this prophecy was fulfilled, that person would be 55 years old at the time of this writing. There is no question that we will not know the day or the hour, but Matthew 24 seems to indicate that we are very, very close to the Messiah's return. The events in the Middle East are surely lining up with this prophecy!

Our response to the war that began on September 11th will indeed echo throughout all eternity.

We have a date with destiny! When we support Israel we are supporting the only nation that was created by an act of God. We are declaring that the Bible is true, that God is not a promise-breaker and that the royal land grant given to Abraham and his seed through Isaac and Jacob was an everlasting and unconditional covenant.

I Will Bless You

There is a selfish reason why we should wholeheartedly support the Jewish people and their beloved country, Israel, but a valid one nonetheless. After promising Abraham that He would make his offspring a great nation, the God of Israel pledged that He would *"bless those who bless you"* (Genesis 12:3). Of course, Abraham's descendants include the Arab people through Ishmael and Esau, and there is every reason for Christians to bless the Arabs today. But we have already seen that God's eternal covenant was passed down to Isaac, Jacob, and the twelve tribes of Israel. This means that the blessing promised by the God of Israel would come to those who particularly blessed the Jewish people.

Ignorant failure or refusal to support the Jews and their right to return to their ancient homeland can cause us to miss the blessings of God. But it can do more than this—it also places us in danger of being cursed by our Creator. God Himself warns humanity of this danger: *"And the one who curses you, I will curse"* (Genesis 12:3) .

By contesting the right of Jews to live in their covenant land, and thereby going against God's holy Word, many are opening themselves up to be cursed! Therefore, anyone who seeks the blessings bestowed by our Heavenly Father should make sure they are obeying His command to bless His special covenant people.

As we have seen, both the Old and New Testaments make abundantly clear that Christians must support Israel in every possible way. This does not mean that the Israeli people and their government are perfect. Far from it: We all are fallen human beings in desperate need of God's grace.

Yet if we touch Jerusalem, which is prophecy, America will lose the blessing of God and America will tragically lose the war on terrorism.

Comfort Israel

"Comfort, yes, comfort My people!"
Says your God.
"Speak comfort to Jerusalem, and cry out to her,
That her warfare is ended,
That her iniquity is pardoned;
For she has received from the LORD's hand
Double for all her sins."

Isaiah 40:1-2

This prophetic word is a God-given mandate to Christians to offer comfort, encouragement, and emotional and financial support to the suffering House of Israel. If this scripture is not for Christians, then for whom? Nation after nation has turned its back on the Jewish people—we cannot do the same.

God said, "Whom shall I send, and who will go for us?" Isaiah cried out, "Here am I; send me." The Lord is saying, "One million praying Christians can win the war that is being fought right now in the land of the Bible. Wake up, the mighty men; wake up, the mighty women! Wake up the Esthers and Nehemiahs!"

But the people who know their God shall be strong, and carry out great exploits.
Daniel 11:32

Israel was not born in 1948. It was born in the heart of God and revealed to Abraham many years before the birth of Isaac. God made a blood covenant with Abraham that the land of Canaan would be given to Abraham's seed through Isaac. (See Genesis 15:18.) As part of that vision, God told Abraham that for 400 years his seed would be strangers in a land that did not belong to them. (See Genesis 15:13.) The seed of Abraham from Isaac spent 400 years in Egypt before Moses led them out, and Israel, the nation, was born.

The word "everlasting" has nothing temporary or conditional about it. It clearly means, "lasting forever." And although Jews are found today in North and South America, Australia, Russia, Europe, many parts of Africa, and virtually every other continent on earth, their historic spiritual and physical center was, and always will be, the Promised Land of Israel.

God's eternal covenant with the descendents of Abraham featured the promise to give them the land of Israel as an everlasting possession. This is recorded in the very first book of the Bible.

I will establish My covenant between Me and you and your descendants after you in their generations, for an everlasting covenant, to be God to you and your descendants after you. Also I give to you and your descendants after you the land in which you are a stranger, all the land of Canaan, as an everlasting possession; and I will be their God."

Genesis 17:7-8

He Will Raise Up Intercessors!

I have set watchmen on your walls, O Jerusalem;
They shall never hold their peace day or night.
You who make mention of the Lord, do not keep silent,
And give Him no rest till He establishes
And till He makes Jerusalem a praise in the earth.

Isaiah 62:6-7

Nothing is more important to God than prayer. God will do nothing without prayer. The fuel that moves the engine of humanity is prayer.

Even as Jeremiah prophesied to the Jewish people during their captivity in Babylon, he was given this promise. The Jews were ultimately delivered from captivity, and revival came to Israel.

"Call to Me, and I will answer you, and show you great and mighty things, which you do not know."

Jeremiah 33:3

Daniel in Babylon refused to obey the decree of the king. The king had decreed that no one could ask any petition of any God or man for thirty days. But Daniel, who prayed three times a day (See Daniel 6:1-23), continued to pray just as he had done before the decree. The God that Daniel was honoring honored Daniel and shut the mouth of the lions in the lions' den. Daniel's prayers prevailed in the midst of Israel's captivity in Babylon.

Darkness flees when we pray! Demons tremble when we pray. Heaven moves when we pray, and angels receive assignments when we pray. Prayer affects three realms: The Divine, the Angelic, and the Human. Without it, demons rule uncontested. (See Ephesians 6.)

We cannot make contact with God without prayer. If we don't make contact with God, no matter how sincere our intentions are, we will not see a change in the circumstances of life.

God has watchmen on the wall. We call them Esthers and Nehemiahs...members of the Jerusalem Prayer Team...people like Corrie ten Boom, and hopefully, people like you.

The world has been scratching its head trying to find an answer to the crisis in the Bible land. That answer is in your hands and mine—we just have to fold them together to get it!

Blow the Trumpet

It is time for Christians to rise up and blow the trumpet! The Church must return to its first love. We must stand in the gap, pay the price, and become watchmen on the wall.

The Bible is filled with stories of believers prevailing in prayer and the Lord winning the battles. You and I can prevail too. The hour is late, but it is not too late to stand in the gap! If prayer was the most effective weapon for Daniel, then prayer must be our most important priority now!

Indeed, America is at war. But if Bible-believing Christians will cry out as Daniel did, then the mouth of the lion will be shut, the fire of the furnace will be quenched, and there will be a Fourth Man walking among us as He walked with Shadrach, Meshach, and Abednego. We can feel the winds of Armageddon blowing strongly in our faces today. The smoke of the Great Tribulation is creeping into the nostrils of every American. The destiny of our nation is at stake.

The question is clear: Will you rise up, put on the armor of God, and do your part in waging America's war?

America's hope lies in those who will not compromise moral principles and biblical values and will commit themselves to the power of prayer!

The Jerusalem Prayer Team

Pray for the peace of Jerusalem.

Psalm 122:6

After sixty-one days of fasting and prayer, God spoke the vision for the Jerusalem Prayer Team in my heart. This was to be God's dream, and God's team. After I heard from Heaven, I flew to Jerusalem to meet with Mayor Ehud Olmert to share the vision of the Jerusalem Prayer Team. He was greatly touched, and flew to Dallas in June 2002 to inaugurate this prayer movement. Dr. Franklin Graham, Dr. Jerry Falwell, former Prime Minister Benjamin Netanyahu, Representative Dick Armey, and Governor Rick Perry were some of those who participated either by letter or video.

Christians from all over America have joined the Jerusalem Prayer Team. Many are household names; i.e., Dr. Tim LaHaye,

Dr. Pat Robertson, Mr. Bill McCartney, Dr. John Maxwell, Mr. Pat Boone, Ms. Kay Arthur, Mrs. Anne Graham Lotz, Rev. Joyce Meyer, Dr. Jerry Falwell, Rev. Tommy Tenney, Dr. Jay Sekulow, Dr. Adrian Rogers, Dr. John Hagee, Dr. Mac Brunson, Dr. Jack Graham, Rev. A. R. Bernard, Dr. Stephen Olford, Rev. Che' An, Dr. Paul Walker, Dr. John Kilpatrick, Pastors Randy and Paula White, Rev. Marilyn Hickey, over 300 national leaders in America, and thousands worldwide.

September 11th, 2001, was a tragic day in American history. It was a physical manifestation of a battle that had been lost weeks, months, and possibly years before because of a lack of prayer. Osama bin Laden had verbally attacked America for years, but the Church was asleep. The demonic powers that were influencing him needed to be violently confronted by holy angels on assignment through the power of prayer—as in the time of Daniel.

I am certain God has raised up Nehemiahs and Esthers to do just that.

The vision of the Jerusalem Prayer Team is to have one million intercessors praying daily for the peace of Jerusalem according to Psalm 122:6. Also pray the prayer of King David who declared: *"Pray for the peace of Jerusalem; they shall prosper that love thee."* Praying for the peace of Jerusalem is not praying for stones or dirt. They don't weep or bleed. It is praying for God's protection over the lives of the citizens of Jerusalem. It is praying for revival. It is praying for God's grace to be poured out on the Bible land, and throughout the Middle East—prayer that demonic powers will be defeated by Holy angels in a battle that cannot be seen with the natural eye.

The pastor of Corrie ten Boom's grandfather went to him and told him that his church was going to pray for the peace of Jerusalem. It inspired the ten Boom family to begin praying weekly. As the Chairman of the Board of Corrie ten Boom House in Haarlem, Holland, we have made the decision to revive this 100-year-old prayer tradition. We are asking for one million Christians to join the Jerusalem Prayer Team, and are asking

100,000 churches to begin praying weekly during their Sunday services for the peace of Jerusalem.

Would you become a Jerusalem Prayer Team member, and would you encourage others to do so? You can email us at jpteam@sbcglobal.net, or write to: The Jerusalem Prayer Team, P.O. Box 910, Euless, TX 76039

The House of Israel is in a state of terror, as are all the children of the Bible land. They need the Lord to answer them in their day of terror. They need the God of Jacob to defend them. They need help from the sanctuary, and strength out of Zion. Now you know my personal prayer, and when it began. I believe one million intercessors praying daily, and 100,000 churches praying weekly for the peace of Jerusalem, will move Heaven and earth.

If you will pray daily, if you will be a part of the Lord's answering this prayer, and a part of touching the destiny of the City of David, then contact me at The Jerusalem Prayer Team, P.O. Box 910, Euless, TX 76039.

The Corrie ten Boom House in Haarlem, Holland, is the center for the Jerusalem Prayer Team in that nation. From there, churches of all nations are being encouraged to pray every Sunday for the peace of Jerusalem.

Corrie would say to the Jews in the hiding place, "Don't worry, angels are around this house. You may not see them, but they are there, protecting you." Not one Jewish person they protected was caught...even the ones in the hiding place escaped after the Nazis came to arrest the ten Boom family.

Over the years, a great number of Jews were hidden in the clock shop, many for just a few days as they headed for Palestine to escape Hitler's ovens. When the Gestapo (the German secret police) raided the house, the entire ten Boom family was taken prisoner.

"It was the last time the ten Boom family would be together... Opa, his children, and one grandson. One hundred years before, almost to the day, in 1844, his father had started a prayer group for the 'peace of Jerusalem.' And now, here they were, arrested for Judenhilfe, helping Jewish people escape Nazi persecution and death."[1]

Casper (84), Betsie (59), and Christiaan (24) died as prisoners. Corrie suffered through prison, but through a miracle, lived to tell the story. Four Jews who were secreted in the hiding place were never caught. They miraculously escaped to safety. Even though the Nazis knew they were there, they couldn't find them.

One of the four was a Jewish rabbi who vowed he would come back, and sing the praises of God. On June 28, 1942, the ten Boom family took him into their home. His name was Meijer Mossel. He was the cantor of the Jewish community in Amsterdam. He told the ten Booms, "I am a chazzen (cantor). Where is my Torah? Where is my Shul (synagogue)? Where is my congregation? The goyim (Gentiles) have laid it all to waste. They have come for the Children of Zion! My only purpose in life is to sing praises to Adonai, the Lord. I am a Yehude, a Yid (one who praises Adonai.)"

In March 1974, he went to Corrie ten Boom's room, and with tears of joy streaming down his face, sang to the Almighty in Hebrew. The rabbi's life had been saved through the power of prayer. To his amazement, Corrie walked into the clock shop. As he walked downstairs, Corrie stood smiling at Meijer Mossel. She had just returned from the filming of the Billy Graham movie, *The Hiding Place.*

For approximately 100 years, from 1844 to 1944, the ten Booms conducted meetings to "pray for the peace of Jerusalem." It is amazing that God would tell me 18 years ago to restore the clock shop. To think that the Lord finally got through my thick skull that prayer, and ONLY prayer, is the key.

Mother Teresa was one of the first people to tell me she would pray daily for the peace of Jerusalem in Rome according to Psalm 122:6. She said to me, "Love is not something you say, it's something you do." I believe that with all my heart. That is why I am appealing to you to join me in seeing what King David saw...what Solomon saw...and what our beloved Lord saw as they prayed in Jerusalem. Each experienced the power of God in Jerusalem—God's glory filled the house where they stood!

"At that time Michael shall stand up,
The great prince who stands watch over the sons of your people;
And there shall be a time of trouble,
Such as never was since there was a nation,
Even to that time.
And at that time your people shall be delivered,
Every one who is found written in the book.
"And many of those who sleep in the dust of the earth shall awake,
Some to everlasting life,
Some to shame and everlasting contempt.
"Those who are wise shall shine
Like the brightness of the firmament,
And those who turn many to righteousness
Like the stars forever and ever.
"But you, Daniel, shut up the words, and seal the book until the time of the
end; many shall run to and fro, and knowledge shall increase."

Daniel 12:1-4 [emphasis in bold added]

Behold, the nations are as a drop in a bucket,
And are counted as the small dust on the scales;...
All nations before Him are as nothing,
And they are counted by Him less than nothing and worthless...
Even the youths shall faint and be weary,
And the young men shall utterly fall,
But those who wait on the LORD
Shall renew their strength;
They shall mount up with wings like eagles,
They shall run and not be weary,
They shall walk and not faint.

Isaiah 40:15,17,30-31

America's hope lies in those who will not compromise moral principles and biblical values and will commit themselves to the power of prayer for the peace of Jerusalem! The Jerusalem Prayer Team began when I resumed the one-hundred-year-prayer meeting in the home of the ten Boom's.

Endnotes

Preface

[1] "America the Target," by Michael D. Evans, *Jerusalem Post*, 30 September 2001.

[2] President George W. Bush, "Address to a Joint Session of Congress and the American People" speech given on 20 September 2001, <http://www.whitehouse.gov/news/releases/2001/09/20010920-8.html> (Accessed 5 April 2003).

[3] The U.S. Secretary of State made this speech to the American Israel Public Affairs Committee's annual policy conference in Washington, 31 March 2003. Transcript courtesy AIPAC.

[4] Israeli Foreign Minister Silvan Shalom made this speech to the American Israel Public Affairs Committee's annual policy conference in Washington, 31 March 2003. Transcript courtesy AIPAC.

[5] Minister Shalom's reference is from Isaiah 50:9.

[6] Italics added. For the complete text of this transmission, please see Appendix A.

Chapter 1: Answering the Wake-Up Call from Hell

[1] On or about May 29, 1998, bin Laden issued a statement entitled "The Nuclear Bomb of Islam," under the banner of the "International Islamic Front for Fighting the Jews and Crusaders," in which he stated that "it is the duty of Muslims to prepare as much force as possible to terrorize the enemies of God," U.S. Department of State, <http://usinfo.state.gov/topical/pol/terror/99129502.htm>

[2] "Before the 1991 Gulf War, Saddam's wealth was estimated at $10 billion by a senior Iraqi defector. But after more than a decade of sanctions, he is no longer as fat a cat. The State Department's Richard Armitage recently put the figure at $7 billion," Adam Zagorin, *Time* magazine, Sunday 2 March 2003.

[3] WASHINGTON, 13 April 2003 (AFP) — U.S. President George W. Bush said Sunday that Syria has chemical weapons, and warned Damascus anew that it "must cooperate" with Washington as it continues its effort to overthrow the Saddam Hussein regime in Iraq.

[4] "Sally's In Syria," *The Mirror*, London, 13 April 2003 — Some of Iraq's top weapons scientists have already fled the country and are in Syria, from where they may seek political safety in France. White House officials said Huda Salih Mahdi Ammash — nicknamed "Chemical Sally" — and Rihab Taha — "Dr. Germ" — both experts in Iraq's biological-weapons program, are in Damascus. Taha is a British-trained microbiologist who led Iraq's drive to cultivate and use deadly anthrax. She is believed to hold vast knowledge about Saddam Hussein's development of weapons of mass destruction. Ammash has been photographed at Saddam's Cabinet meetings, and at a meeting with his son, Qusai, who ran most of Iraq's military and security organizations.

[5] "France urges U.S., U.K. to ensure Iraqis' security," by Paul Taylor, CAIRO, 12 April 2003 (Reuters) — France urged the United States and Britain on Saturday to ensure security for the Iraqi people after scenes of looting and lawlessness following the fall of President Saddam Hussein.... Villepin and Maher stressed

the urgency of reviving Middle East peace efforts through the publication of a "Road Map" to a Palestinian state, drawn up by the United States, the European Union, Russia, and the United Nations.... He said France was willing to contribute to an international military presence to observe a cease-fire and to host a conference to provide an international framework for peace, once the first stages of the "Road Map" had been implemented.

[6] "Latest bin Laden Tape Release," by BBC NEWS Tuesday, 08 April 2003, at 03:56 a.m. — An audio recording said to be of Osama bin Laden has emerged in which he urges Muslims to rise up against their governments that support the war on Iraq.... In February 2003, an audiotape purporting to be by bin Laden called for attacks on U.S. and British targets if Iraq was invaded.

[7] On October 7, 1985, one of the P.L.O.'s factions, the Palestine Liberation Front, hijacked the Italian cruise ship *Achille Lauro* and demanded the release of Palestinian prisoners held in Israel. Egyptian President Hosni Mubarak persuaded the hijackers to surrender and allowed the PLF leader, Muhammad Abbas, and the other terrorists to fly to Tunisia. President Ronald Reagan sent U.S. warplanes to intercept the flight, however, and forced it to land at a U.S.-Italian air base in Sicily. The United States and Italy fought over jurisdiction in the case, but the Italians refused to extradite any of the men.

[8] "Fighting Terrorism," by Benjamin Netanyahu; Noonday Press (March 1997). The quote is attributed to Abdel Rahman by his follower, Egyptian immigrant El Sayyid Nosair, who was charged with murdering Rabbi Meir Kahane in New York on 1 November 1990. Police found 47 boxes of papers in his home, mostly in Arabic, but assumed they were religious materials. They were later found to contain instructions on how to conduct assassinations and attacks on aircraft, as well as formulas for making bombs.

[9] Ibid.

[10] Steven Emerson's 1994 PBS documentary, "Jihad in America," warned that militant Islam was organizing inside America.

[11] President George W. Bush, in a graduation speech at West Point Military Academy, New York, 1 June 2002.

[12] Address by Israeli Foreign Minister Silvan Shalom to the AIPAC Policy Conference, Washington, D.C., 30 March 2003.

Chapter 2: A War of Biblical Proportions

[1] "U.S. Troops Enter Tikrit with Only 'Light Resistance,'" *The Washington Post*, 14 April 2003 — Iraq has the world's second-largest proven crude reserves, at 112 billion barrels, but its pipelines, pumping stations, and oil reservoirs have suffered for years from a dearth of funds and lack of maintenance. In recent years, oil has accounted for 95 percent of Iraq's revenue, an estimated $22 billion a year.

[2] "The U.S. administration wants to destroy Iraq in order to control the Middle East oil, and consequently control the politics as well as the oil and economic policies of the whole world." — Saddam Hussein in a letter to the United Nations, 19 September 2002.

[3] Kenneth M. Pollack, "Why Iraq Can't Be Deterred," *The New York Times*, 26 September 2002.

[4] Sharon told Israel Television Channel 2 that Israel has information that "weapons he [Iraqi leader Saddam Hussein] wanted to hide, chemical weapons, biological weapons, were indeed transferred to Syria."

[5] "If Attacked, Israel Might Nuke Iraq," by Ze'ev Schiff, *Haaretz*, 15 August 2002.

[6] "North Korea's Missile Export Mischief," *The New York Times*, 12 December 2002, and Uri Dan, "Yemen's Scuds Baghdad-Bound," *New York Post*, 27 December 2002.

[7] "Iraqi rockets sent to Syria for use by Hizbullah," by Ze'ev Schiff, *Haaretz*, 12 June 2002.

Chapter 3: The Line Drawn in the Sand

[1] Abram, later Abraham, lived during the period 2000—1500 B.C. The account of what happened at Babel (Babylon), with its anti-God dictator, its organized rebellion against God, and its refusal to believe God's promise to the Jewish people through Abraham, bears a striking resemblance to present events.

[2] "And another angel followed, saying, *"Babylon is fallen, is fallen, that great city, because she has made all nations drink of the wine of the wrath of her fornication"* (Revelation 14:8). This passage follows two earlier scriptures that bear witness to a similar message: *"Babylon is fallen, is fallen"* (Isaiah 20:9), contains precisely the same words as found in the second angel's message which prophesies the destruction of spiritual Babylon; also, the wine of Babylon's fornication was also found in literal Babylon: *"Babylon hath been a golden cup in the Lord's hand, that made all the earth drunken: the nations have drunken of her wine; therefore the nations are mad"* (Jeremiah 51:7 KJV).

[3] "Women are not allowed to drive vehicles or ride bicycles on public roads"; U.S. State Department, Consular Information Sheet for Saudi Arabia, 16 December 1996.

[4] In Islam, eating pork is said to contribute to lack of morality and shame, plus greed for wealth, dirtiness, and gluttony. Muslims are forbidden by God to eat pork. This is detailed in some of the verses in the Koran. An exemplary verse: "He has only forbidden you dead meat, and blood, and the flesh of swine, and any food over which the name of other than Allah has been invoked." According to Islam, pigs' bodies contain many toxins, worms, latent diseases, and excessive quantities of histamine and imidazole. (The Royal Embassy of Saudi Arabia, Washington, D.C.)

[5] The Ka'ba, the most sacred building of Islam, is located in the center of the Holy Mosque in Mecca. It is a tall, rectangular, box-like structure 15 m high with sides measuring 10.5 m by 12 m. The Black Stone (possibly from a meteorite) is built into the eastern corner of the structure, along a stone known as Hajar as'ad (the lucky stone) which is touched by pilgrims (hajis) during their circumambulation. Outside the northwest side there is a low semicircular wall which encloses an area known as the Hijr which is believed to mark the burial place of Ismail and his mother Hajar. The Ka'ba is built of large blue-gray granite blocks set in mortar resting on a base of marble. The entrance is on the

northeast side and is 2 m above ground level (it is reached by a portable set of wooden steps). Inside the Ka'ba there are three tall wooden pillars which support the wooden roof which can be reached by a wooden ladder. The floor is made of marble and the ceiling is covered with cloth hangings.

According to Muslim tradition the Ka'ba was built by Ibrahim and Ismail and was the first sanctuary established on Earth. This early building was simply a rectangular unroofed enclosure the height of a man. Idols were housed within the Ka'ba, the most prominent of whom were al-Lat, al-Uzza and al-Manat. Three hundred and sixty idols were arranged in a circle outside the Ka'ba forming a sacred area (Haram) where no blood could be shed. In 629 after a period of exile Muhammad conquered Mecca but left the form of the Ka'ba unaltered (except for the removal of idols). The outside of the structure is covered with a huge cloth of fabric (kiswa) which is replaced annually. (Andrew Petersen, *Dictionary of Islamic Architecture* (Routledge, 1996)

[6] Muslims believe their Id al-Adha (Feast of the Sacrifice) commemorates God's sparing Abraham's son, Ishmael, after the patriarch was about to sacrifice him to prove his faith. Jews and Christians believe it was Abraham's younger son, Isaac, who was saved. A modern Islamic interpretation of the festival is "that all mankind should unite on the fundamental principles of religion revealed to it, and live as one brotherhood with equality for all. But that is only possible through a sacrifice of one's animal desires, which are the cause of all discord and enmity among people." *(The Light & Islamic Review*, January-February 1992, pp. 4-6.)

[7] "Music has traditionally been one of the more controversial issues in the Muslim world. While all Muslim scholars have always accepted and even encouraged chanting the call to prayer and the Qur'an, the permissibility of other forms of music, especially instrumental music, has been problematic. In Arabic, the word *musiqa*, which is translated as music, even has a more narrow sense than does the English word music. *Musiqa* in Arabic refers mainly to popular and instrumental music and excludes genres such as Qur'anic chanting and the Muslim call to prayer (adh'an)… In spite of critiques such as this, many forms of music have traditionally been present in the Muslim world and are still found throughout it today." (Prof. Alan Godlas, *Islam and Islamic Studies*, The University of Georgia, 2003).

Chapter 4: Jihad: A Truly Unholy War

[1] Koran, Sura 2:193.

[2] This story of Muhammad is part of Islamic tradition:
"When Muhammad and his followers were about to attack Mecca to subjugate it to Islam, his adherents arrested Abu Sufyan, one of Mecca's inhabitants. They brought him to Muhammad. Muhammad told him: "Woe to you, O Abu Sufyan. Is it not time for you to realize that there is no God but the only God?" Abu Sufyan answered: "I do believe that." Muhammad then said to him: "Woe to you, O Abu Sufyan. Is it not time for you to know that I am the apostle of God?" Abu Sufyan answered: "By God, O Muhammad, of this there is doubt in my soul." The Abbas who was present with Muhammad told Abu Sufyan:

"Woe to you! Accept Islam and testify that Muhammad is the apostle of God before your neck is cut off by the sword." Thus he professed the faith of Islam and became a Muslim." (Of the many sources which record this story: Ibn Hisham, part 4, p. 11 ("Biography of the Prophet"); "The Chronicle of the Tabari," part 2, p. 157; Ibn Kathir, "The Prophetic Biography," part 3, p. 549, and "The Beginning and the End.")

[3] For a discussion of this concept, see Alan Caruba, "Islam: The Endless Jihad," 26 September 2001, on the Web site: The National Anxiety Center (<anxiety-center.com/warning.htm>).

[4] "The defeat of the Saracen invaders of Frankish lands at Tours (more properly Poitiers) in 732 A.D. was a turning point in history. It is not likely the Muslims, if victorious, would have penetrated, at least at once, far into the north, but they would surely have seized South Gaul, and thence readily have crushed the weak Christian powers of Italy." From: William Stearns Davis, ed., Readings in Ancient History: Illustrative Extracts from the Sources, 2 Vols. (Boston: Allyn and Bacon, 1912-13), Vol. II: Rome and the West, pp. 362-364.

[5] The siege of Vienna in 1683 was the last major threat to the West from Islam and established the balance of power in Eastern Europe and the Balkans down to the end of World War I. For a definitive work on the subject, see: John Stoye, *The Siege of Vienna*, New Edition (Birlinn, 2001).

[6] Arab countries hold 60 percent of global oil reserves and 25 percent of global gas reserves. (Source: World Economic Forum, Arab World Competitiveness Meeting, 9 September 2002.)

[7] "The United States has become increasingly dependent on imported energy, and there has been an attendant impact on the balance of payments. For example, 43 percent of the oil used in the United States was imported in the first six months of 1979, compared with 35 percent in 1973. Of these 1979 imports, 67 percent was supplied by the OPEC countries, including 40 percent from Arab producers. During the six months preceding the 1973-74 embargo, Arab producers supplied only 15 percent of U.S. imported oil. At the same time, OPEC oil has increased in price, through the machinations of the cartel. The massive income transfer is indicated by the rise in the U.S. oil balance of payments bill, from $3.4 billion in the first six months of 1973 to $24.4 billion during the first six months of 1979." In: "Supplemental Sources of Natural Gas: An Economic Comparison," by Alan Kaufman, Congressional Research Service, and Susan J. Bodilly, Rand Corporation, Washington, D.C., October 1981.

[8] The Arab world refers to Israeli Independence Day on 15 May 1948 as "*Nakba* [catastrophe] Day," because it describes their armies' failure to destroy the newborn Jewish state. The Palestinians refer to Israeli independence as a *nakba*, in contrast to their failure to create their own state in Palestine, in accordance with the 1947 U.N. General Assembly Resolution 181 on the partition of Palestinian into two states, Jewish and Arab, linked by an economic union. So far only two Arab countries, Egypt and Jordan, have beaten the sword of *nakba* into the plowshare of peaceful coexistence.

Chapter 5: A Further Distorted Islam

[1] Fact Sheet: The Charges against International Terrorist usama bin Laden; released by the Bureau of South Asian Affairs, U.S. Department of State, Washington, D.C.; 20 January 2001.

[2] Britain performed an eventually even higher elevation—with more oil—by utilizing its mandate under the newly created League of Nations following World War I to create the state of Iraq. The league awarded "mandates" over Iraq, Palestine, and Transjordan to Britain, and over Lebanon and Syria to France. Iraq's boundaries were fixed by Britain by combining three provinces of the former Ottoman Empire—Mosul, Baghdad, and Basra—into a new political entity.

[3] "Since the September 11 attacks, perpetrated by people who mostly came from Saudi Arabia, "Wahabism" has entered the vocabulary of American policy makers almost as synonymous with death, destruction, and terror. Moreover, Wahabi teachings and influence in Riyadh have colored the American image of Saudi Arabia, threatening to move it from the category of a friend helping to stabilize oil prices and the region to one of a foe alien to American values and bent on hurting Americans," from "Don't play into the hands of extremists," by Youssef M. Ibrahim, *The International Herald Tribune*, 12 August 2002.

[4] "Wahabism…is a strain of Islam that emerged not during the Crusades, nor even at the time of the anti-Turkish wars of the 17th century, but less than two centuries ago. It is violent, it is intolerant, and it is fanatical beyond measure. It originated in Arabia, and it is the official theology of the Gulf states. Wahabism is the most extreme form of Islamic fundamentalism. Not all Muslims are suicide bombers, but all Muslim suicide bombers are Wahabis—except, perhaps, for some disciples of atheist Leftists posing as Muslims in the interests of personal power, such as Yasser Arafat or Saddam Hussein." Steven Schwartz, "This business all began in Saudi Arabia," in *The Spectator*, 23 September 2001.

[5] Contrary to Palestinian claims, the visit of then Israeli opposition leader Ariel Sharon to Jerusalem's Temple Mount in late September 2000 did not cause the outbreak of Palestinian violence. Rather, the wave of terrorism was the result of a strategic Palestinian decision to use violence—rather than negotiation—as the primary instrument of advancing their political cause. Palestinian officials themselves divulged this fact in statements they made in the Arabic-language media. On 6 December 2000, the semi-official Palestinian daily *Al-Ayyam* reported: "Speaking at a symposium in Gaza, Palestinian Minister of Communications Imad Al-Falouji, confirmed that the Palestinian Authority had begun preparations for the outbreak of the current Intifada from the moment the Camp David talks concluded, this in accordance with instructions given by Chairman Arafat himself. Mr. Falouji went on to state that Arafat launched this Intifada as a culminating stage to the immutable Palestinian stance in the negotiations, and was not meant merely as a protest of Israeli opposition leader Ariel Sharon's visit to the Temple Mount."

[6] "At least 200 Palestinians suspected of collaborating with Israel are being held in Palestinian Authority prisons, according to informed Palestinian sources....

Yesterday members of Fatah's military wing, the Aksa Martyrs Brigades, shot and killed a mother of seven in Tulkarm after accusing her of collaborating with Israel. Ikhlas Yasin, 39, was shot in the town's main square.

Palestinians in the city told the Post that her son, who had been kidnapped earlier by Fatah gunmen, had confessed that his mother had helped the Israeli security forces in killing Ziad Da'as, a wanted member of the Brigades.

At least 14 Palestinians have been killed in Tulkarm over the past three months on charges of collaboration with Israel. More than 60 Palestinians from the West Bank and Gaza Strip have been killed since the beginning of the intifada for allegedly helping Israel's Shin Bet security service. The PA executed at least five others for the same reason." From: "Fatah executes Tulkarm mother of 7," by Khaled Abu Toameh, *Jerusalem Post*, Sunday, 25 August 2002.

[7] "Another body of opinion holds that a U.S. victory over Saddam Hussein will revive hope for peace in the Middle East. In the view of Professor Robert Lieber of Georgetown University, 'The road to Jerusalem goes through Baghdad, not vice versa. The ouster of Saddam will have very beneficial effects in fostering an Arab-Israeli peace process.'

Lieber argues that removing Saddam would eliminate a key source of support for Palestinian terrorism and obstructionism. It would further enhance U.S. power and influence in the Middle East—an outcome that could make peace between Israel and the Arabs more likely. After all, the U.S. victory in 1991 led Israel and its adversaries to sit down and talk peace. 'It was the Gulf War and the defeat of Saddam Hussein in 1991 that made that possible,' Lieber said." From: "What Would Defeating Saddam Trigger?" by William Schneider, American Enterprise Institute for Public Policy Research, 23 November 2002.

[8] Mike Evans, "Islam and the Infidels," *Jerusalem Post*, 5 September 2002, p. 9.

[9] Sheikh Prof. Abdul Hadi Palazzi, Secretary General of the Italian Moslem Association and Moslem co-chair of the Islam-Israel Fellowship of the Root and Branch Association, noted: "'It is the Wahabi sect, that rules Saudi Arabia, that is responsible for the politicized Islam so dominant in the Middle East and throughout much of the Islamic world.' He calls the Wahabis, once a tribe of Beduin nomads, 'primitive literalists'—a case in point is the two Saudi princes who accompanied astronauts on a NASA mission ten years ago, in order to give official witness before a religious court that the earth was, in truth, not flat—and asserts that the Wahabis have made tremendous efforts to transform Islam from a religion into a totalitarian political ideology." From: "For Allah's sake," by Abigail Radoszkowicz, *Jerusalem Post International Edition*, 16 February 2001.

[10] "This indoctrination consists of the rawest incitement to murder, as in this sermon by Arafat-appointed and Arafat-funded Ahmad Abu Halabiya broadcast live on official Palestinian Authority television early in the Intifada. The subject is 'the Jews.' (Note: not the Israelis, but the Jews.) 'They must be butchered and killed, as Allah the Almighty said: 'Fight them: Allah will torture them at your hands.'... Have no mercy on the Jews....Wherever you meet them, kill them.'"

The rationale for such murderous behavior is taught not just in Palestine, but throughout the Arab world. On March 10, an article in the Saudi newspaper *al-Riyadh* described in rich detail how the Jews ritually slaughter Christian and Muslim children to use their blood in their holiday foods. It explained that for one holiday (Purim), the Jew must kill an adolescent, but for Passover, the victim must be 10 years or younger." From: "Arafat Is Headmaster for Suicide Bombers," by Charles Krauthammer, *New York Daily News*, Editorial, 27 March 2002.

[11] "Saddam Hussein has distributed $260,000 to 26 families of Palestinians killed in attacks on Israel, including $25,000 awarded to the family of a Hamas suicide bomber. In a packed banquet hall on Wednesday, the families came one-by-one to receive $10,000 checks. A large banner said: 'The Arab Ba'ath Party Welcomes the Families of the Martyrs for the Distribution of Blessings of Saddam Hussein.'"

"...Saddam gives $10,000 to the families of those killed within 30 days of death, and $25,000 to the families of suicide bombers.

"In total, Saddam has given more than $35 million to West Bank and Gaza Strip families of Palestinians killed during the fighting, said Ibrahim Zanen, spokesman for the Arab Liberation Front in Gaza." From: "Saddam rewards Palestinian 'Martyrs'" by Hassan Fattah, The Associated Press, 14 March 2003.

Chapter 6: The Sword's Edge: The Palestinian Liberation Organization

[1] "America the Target," by Mike Evans, *Jerusalem Post*, 30 September 2001, p. 6.

[2] Dr. George Habash was the founder and secretary general of the People's Front for the Liberation of Palestine. Nayef Hawatmeh is secretary general of the Democratic Front for the Liberation of Palestine.

[3] *Al-Hawadeth*, 11 July 1975.

[4] Ibid.

[5] *Time* magazine.

[6] *Los Angeles Times*, 21 January 1976.

[7] "Penetrating Terrorist Networks," David Ignatius, Washington Post.com, Sunday, 16 September 2001, p. B07#.

[8] Quoted in "The Forgotten Terrorist," by Thomas W. Murphy, *USA In Review*, February 27, 2003—"He is one of the world's most notorious terrorists, responsible for the deaths of thousands of men, women, and children. He's plied his trade in Europe, Africa, and the Middle East. Bombings, hijackings, and assassination; he's mastered them all. The United States has enough evidence to indict him for the kidnapping and brutal murder of two American diplomats. The United States knows his exact location. The United States can arrest him and bring him to justice whenever it chooses. His name is Muhammad Abd ar-Rauf al-Qudwah al-Husayni, better known as Yasser Arafat."

[9] Task Force on Terrorism and Unconventional Warfare, U.S. House of Representatives, Washington, D.C. 20515; Eric Cantor, Virginia, chairman; "Arafat—Never a Partner for Peace," 16 November 2001.

Chapter 7: A Blood-Soaked History; A Blood-Soaked Future

[1] "Fatah is sending hundreds of Palestinian suicide bombers from Lebanon to launch attacks on American and British troops in Iraq, according to Col. Munir

Maqdah, one of the top Fatah officials in Lebanon. Maqdah told Agence France Press on Wednesday that hundreds of Palestinians have already been sent to Iraq on suicide missions. He said the would-be suicide bombers belong to Fatah's Popular Army that operates in Palestinian refugee camps in Lebanon. The secretary-general of Fatah in Lebanon, Sultan Abu Aynain, urged Syria and Lebanon to allow Palestinian volunteers to travel to Iraq. "I call on Presidents Emil Lahoud [of Lebanon] and Bashar Assad [of Syria] to open their borders before the martyrdom fighters in the refugee camps in order to defend Iraq against the American-British invasion," he said at a Fatah rally in the Rashidiyeh refugee camp in south Lebanon. 'The people of Iraq are being slaughtered while the Arab nation has sold itself to the American-Zionist Satan," he added.

Fatah is the first Palestinian group to announce that it is dispatching suicide bombers to Iraq. Earlier this week Islamic Jihad, which claimed responsibility for Sunday's suicide bombing in Netanya, said the first wave of its 'martyrdom seekers' has already arrived in Iraq.

On Monday, some 30 Palestinian volunteers from Lebanon headed for Iraq to join the Iraqi army in fighting against the American and British forces, according to Palestinian sources, who said the volunteers managed to enter Iraq from neighboring Syria.

The sources added that several Palestinian radical groups based in Syria have also started recruiting suicide bombers to be sent to Iraq. At least 10 different Palestinian factions, some affiliated with Iran and Libya, operate out of Syria, which provide them with military bases and weapons." From: "Fatah Confirms Sending Suicide Bombers to Iraq," by Khaled Abu Toameh and Douglas Davis, *Jerusalem Post*, 3 April 2003.

[2] "Suicide Blast Shows Newest Danger on Front Lines," *The New York Times*, 29 March 2003.

[3] "Saddam Rewards Bomber's Family," by Almin Karamehmedovic, The Associated Press, 12 April 2003.

[4] Ibid.

[5] Ibid.

[6] Netanyahu, Benjamin (Binyamin), U.S. House of Representatives Government Reform Committee, 11 September 2001.

Chapter 8: The Road Through Baghdad Leads to Jerusalem

[1] "Letter to an Anti-Zionist Friend," Rev. Martin Luther King Jr., *The Saturday Review*, XLVII (August 1967), p. 76.

[2] Prime Minister's Statement on Middle East Peace Process, 10 Downing Street, 14 March 2003.

[3] President Bush, Prime Minister Blair Hold Press Availability; Camp David, Maryland; 27 March 2003 (White House transcript).

[4] Ibid.

[5] "Holding Jesus Hostage," by Mike Evans, *The Jerusalem Post International Edition*, 16 May 2002, p. 15.

[6] For the complete text of the Quartet's Road Map, see Appendix A.

[7] Abbas attempted to refute what he called "the Zionist fantasy, the fantastic lie that six million Jews were killed" in the Holocaust in his 1983 book, *The Other Side: The Secret Relations Between Nazism and the Leadership of the Zionist Movement.* It was originally his doctoral dissertation, completed at Moscow's Oriental College. (Translated from the Arabic by the Simon Wiesenthal Center in Los Angeles.)

[8] "Bush Says Pleased with New Palestinian Leader," Hillsborough, Northern Ireland, (Reuters), 8 April 2003.

[9] "Peres presents peace plan," by Joshua Brilliant, United Press International, Tel Aviv, 18 May 2002.

Chapter 9: What Lies Ahead for the U.S.?

[1] George Santayana, *The Life of Reason,* Volume 1, 1905.

[2] The Jerusalem Embassy Act of 1995 (U.S. Senate Bill "S. 1332"; Public Law 104-45; 104th Congress an Act, states, inter alia: "To provide for the relocation of the United States Embassy in Israel to Jerusalem, The Congress makes the following findings:

    (1) Each sovereign nation, under international law and custom, may designate its own capital.

    (2) Since 1950, the city of Jerusalem has been the capital of the State of Israel.

    (3) The city of Jerusalem is the seat of Israel's President, Parliament, and Supreme Court, and the site of numerous govement ministries and social and cultural institutions.

    (4) The city of Jerusalem is the spiritual center of Judaism, and is also considered a holy city by the members of other religious faiths.

    (5) From 1948-1967, Jerusalem was a divided city and Israeli citizens of all faiths as well as Jewish citizens of all states were denied access to holy sites in the area controlled by Jordan.

    (6) In 1967, the city of Jerusalem was reunited during the conflict known as the Six Day War.

    (7) Since 1967, Jerusalem has been a united city administered by Israel, and persons of all religious faiths have been guaranteed full access to holy sites within the city...

Every six months, U.S. presidents have routinely issued the required waiver statement to deprive the above bill of any practical impact.

[3] "Some Western analysts believe that by the late 1980s Syria had armed many of its modern missiles, including Scuds, with chemical warheads. Currently, Syria's strategic chemical weapons stockpile is primarily composed of the nerve agent sarin. However, recent reports indicate that Syria has successfully produced the much more persistent nerve agent VX, and that it has tested missile warheads armed with VX." From: "Syria's Scuds and Chemical Weapons," by Eric Croddy, Center for Nonproliferation Studies, Monterey Institute for International Studies, March 1999.

Chapter 10: The Wake-Up Call from Heaven: Preparing for Our Lord's Coming!

[1] Hans Poley, *Return to the Hiding Place* (Elgin: Chariot Family Publishers, 1993), p. 147. Mr. Poley was the first person hidden by the ten Boom family.

Appendix A

OFFICIAL:

"A Performance-Based Roadmap to a Permanent Two-State Solution to the Israeli-Palestinian Conflict"

The document below is the official "Road Map" plan.

Is there a difference between the "UNCLASSIFIED" Road Map plan; the draft that printed from my fax machine a few days after the speeches by Secretary of State Powell and Foreign Minister Shalom, before Abbas was confirmed; and the Official Road Map? In substance, no there is not.

They both call for

1. official recognition of a Palestine state (P.L.O. state)

2. East Jerusalem as the Capital

3. all lands taken in 1967 that are Occupied to be returned

4. UN resolutions 242/338/1397 to be complied with

5. the Quartet to facilitate the implementation and monitoring of the plan

6. Israel to sign a Peace Treaty with two terrorist states, Syria and Lebanon, and a family of terrorist organizations represented by the P.L.O.

7. Israel to freeze all settlement activities and hold that Jews have no right to live in, what they term the Occupied territory and must move out of biblical Judea and Samaria

8. Israel not to demolish any homes (even those of suspected terrorists)

9. the P.L.O. be allowed to come back into East Jerusalem and establish institutions now

10. Palestine refugees to be allowed to return

11. the world Quartet-hosted conference to take place

(Released April 30, 2003)

The following is a performance-based and goal-driven roadmap, with clear phases, timelines, target dates, and benchmarks aiming at progress through reciprocal steps by the two parties in the political, security, economic, humanitarian, and institution-building fields, under the auspices of the Quartet [the United States, European Union, United Nations, and Russia]. The destination is a final and comprehensive settlement of the Israel-Palestinian conflict by 2005, as presented in President Bush's speech of 24 June, and welcomed by the EU, Russia and the UN in the 16 July and 17 September Quartet Ministerial statements.

A two-state solution to the Israeli-Palestinian conflict will only be achieved through an end to violence and terrorism, when the Palestinian people have a leadership acting decisively against terror and willing and able to build a practicing democracy based on tolerance and liberty, and through Israel's readiness to do what is necessary for a democratic Palestinian state to be established, and a clear, unambiguous acceptance by both parties of the goal of a negotiated settlement as described below. The Quartet will assist and facilitate implementation of the plan, starting in Phase I, including direct discussions between the parties as required. The plan establishes a realistic timeline for implementation. However, as a performance-based plan, progress will require and depend upon the good faith efforts of the parties, and their compliance with each of the obligations outlined below. Should the parties perform their obligations rapidly, progress within and through the phases may come sooner than indicated in the plan. Non-compliance with obligations will impede progress.

A settlement, negotiated between the parties, will result in the emergence of an independent, democratic, and viable Palestinian state living side by side in peace and security with Israel and its other neighbors. The settlement will resolve the Israel-Palestinian conflict, and end the occupation that began in 1967, based on the foundations of the Madrid Conference, the principle of land for peace, UNSCRs 242, 338 and 1397, agreements previously reached by the parties, and the initiative of Saudi Crown Prince Abdullah – endorsed by the Beirut Arab League Summit – calling for acceptance of Israel as a neighbor living in peace and security, in the context of a comprehensive settlement. This initiative is a vital element of international efforts to promote a comprehensive peace on all tracks, including the Syrian-Israeli and Lebanese-Israeli tracks.

The Quartet will meet regularly at senior levels to evaluate the parties' performance on implementation of the plan. In each phase, the parties are expected to perform their obligations in parallel, unless otherwise indicated.

Phase I: Ending Terror and Violence, Normalizing Palestinian Life, and Building Palestinian Institutions – Present to May 2003

In Phase I, the Palestinians immediately undertake an unconditional cessation of violence according to the steps outlined below; such action should be accompanied by supportive measures undertaken by Israel. Palestinians and Israelis resume security cooperation based on the Tenet work plan to end violence, terrorism, and incitement through restructured and effective Palestinian security services. Palestinians undertake comprehensive political reform in preparation for statehood, including drafting a Palestinian constitution, and free, fair and open elections upon the basis of those measures. Israel takes all necessary steps to help normalize Palestinian life. Israel withdraws from Palestinian areas occupied from September 28, 2000 and the two sides restore the status quo that existed at that time, as security performance and cooperation progress. Israel also freezes all settlement activity, consistent with the Mitchell report.

At the outset of Phase I:

- Palestinian leadership issues unequivocal statement reiterating Israel's right to exist in peace and security and calling for an immediate and unconditional ceasefire to end armed activity and all acts of violence against Israelis anywhere. All official Palestinian institutions end incitement against Israel.

- Israeli leadership issues unequivocal statement affirming its commitment to the two-state vision of an independent, viable, sovereign Palestinian state living in peace and security alongside Israel, as expressed by President Bush, and calling for an immediate end to violence against Palestinians everywhere. All official Israeli institutions end incitement against Palestinians.

Security

- Palestinians declare an unequivocal end to violence and terrorism and undertake visible efforts on the ground to arrest, disrupt, and restrain individuals and groups conducting and planning violent attacks on Israelis anywhere.

- Rebuilt and refocused Palestinian Authority security apparatus begins sustained, targeted, and effective operations aimed at confronting all those engaged in terror and dismantlement of terrorist capabilities and infrastructure. This includes commencing confiscation of illegal weapons and consolidation of security authority, free of association with terror and corruption.

- GOI takes no actions undermining trust, including deportations, attacks on civilians; confiscation and/or demolition of Palestinian homes and property, as a punitive measure or to facilitate Israeli construction; destruction of Palestinian institutions and infrastructure; and other measures specified in the Tenet work plan.

- Relying on existing mechanisms and on-the-ground resources, Quartet representatives begin informal monitoring and consult with the parties on establishment of a formal monitoring mechanism and its implementation.

- Implementation, as previously agreed, of U.S. rebuilding, training and resumed security cooperation plan in collaboration with outside oversight board (U.S.–Egypt–Jordan). Quartet support for efforts to achieve a lasting, comprehensive cease-fire.

  - All Palestinian security organizations are consolidated into three services reporting to an empowered Interior Minister.

  - Restructured/retrained Palestinian security forces and IDF counterparts progressively resume security cooperation and other undertakings in implementation of the Tenet work plan, including regular senior-level meetings, with the participation of U.S. security officials.

- Arab states cut off public and private funding and all other forms of support for groups supporting and engaging in violence and terror.

- All donors providing budgetary support for the Palestinians channel these funds through the Palestinian Ministry of Finance's Single Treasury Account.

- As comprehensive security performance moves forward, IDF withdraws progressively from areas occupied since September 28, 2000 and the two sides restore the status quo that existed prior to September 28, 2000. Palestinian security forces redeploy to areas vacated by IDF.

Palestinian Institution-Building

- Immediate action on credible process to produce draft constitution for Palestinian statehood. As rapidly as possible, constitutional committee circulates draft Palestinian constitution, based on strong parliamentary democracy and cabinet with empowered prime minister, for public comment/debate. Constitutional committee proposes draft document for submission after elections for approval by appropriate Palestinian institutions.

- Appointment of interim prime minister or cabinet with empowered executive authority/decision-making body.
- GOI fully facilitates travel of Palestinian officials for PLC and Cabinet sessions, internationally supervised security retraining, electoral and other reform activity, and other supportive measures related to the reform efforts.
- Continued appointment of Palestinian ministers empowered to undertake fundamental reform. Completion of further steps to achieve genuine separation of powers, including any necessary Palestinian legal reforms for this purpose.
- Establishment of independent Palestinian election commission. PLC reviews and revises election law.
- Palestinian performance on judicial, administrative, and economic benchmarks, as established by the International Task Force on Palestinian Reform.
- As early as possible, and based upon the above measures and in the context of open debate and transparent candidate selection/electoral campaign based on a free, multi-party process, Palestinians hold free, open, and fair elections.
- GOI facilitates Task Force election assistance, registration of voters, movement of candidates and voting officials. Support for NGOs involved in the election process.
- GOI reopens Palestinian Chamber of Commerce and other closed Palestinian institutions in East Jerusalem based on a commitment that these institutions operate strictly in accordance with prior agreements between the parties.

Humanitarian Response
- Israel takes measures to improve the humanitarian situation. Israel and Palestinians implement in full all recommendations of the Bertini report to improve humanitarian conditions, lifting curfews and easing restrictions on movement of

persons and goods, and allowing full, safe, and unfettered access of international and humanitarian personnel.

- AHLC reviews the humanitarian situation and prospects for economic development in the West Bank and Gaza and launches a major donor assistance effort, including to the reform effort.
- GOI and PA continue revenue clearance process and transfer of funds, including arrears, in accordance with agreed, transparent monitoring mechanism.

Civil Society

- Continued donor support, including increased funding through PVOs/NGOs, for people to people programs, private sector development and civil society initiatives.

Settlements

- GOI immediately dismantles settlement outposts erected since March 2001.
- Consistent with the Mitchell Report, GOI freezes all settlement activity (including natural growth of settlements).

Phase II: Transition — June 2003-December 2003

In the second phase, efforts are focused on the option of creating an independent Palestinian state with provisional borders and attributes of sovereignty, based on the new constitution, as a way station to a permanent status settlement. As has been noted, this goal can be achieved when the Palestinian people have a leadership acting decisively against terror, willing and able to build a practicing democracy based on tolerance and liberty. With such a leadership, reformed civil institutions and security structures, the Palestinians will have the active support of the Quartet and the broader international community in establishing an independent, viable, state. Progress into Phase II will be based upon the consensus judgment of the Quartet of whether conditions are appropriate to proceed, taking into account performance of both parties. Furthering and sustaining efforts to normalize Palestinian lives and build Palestinian institutions, Phase II starts after Palestinian elections and ends with possible creation of an independent Palestinian state with provisional borders in 2003. Its primary goals are continued comprehensive security performance and effective security cooperation, continued normalization of Palestinian life and institution-building, further building on and sustaining of the goals outlined in Phase I, ratification of a democratic Palestinian constitution, formal establishment of office of prime minister, consolidation of political reform, and the creation of a Palestinian state with provisional borders.

- **International Conference:** Convened by the Quartet, in consultation with the parties, immediately after the successful conclusion of Palestinian elections, to support Palestinian economic recovery and launch a process, leading to establishment of an independent Palestinian state with provisional borders.

  - Such a meeting would be inclusive, based on the goal of a comprehensive Middle East peace (including between Israel and Syria, and Israel and Lebanon), and based on the principles described in the preamble to this document.

  - Arab states restore pre-intifada links to Israel (trade offices, etc.).

  - Revival of multilateral engagement on issues including regional water resources, environment, economic development, refugees, and arms control issues.

- New constitution for democratic, independent Palestinian state is finalized and approved by appropriate Palestinian institutions. Further elections, if required, should follow approval of the new constitution.

- Empowered reform cabinet with office of prime minister formally established, consistent with draft constitution.

- Continued comprehensive security performance, including effective security cooperation on the bases laid out in Phase I.

- Creation of an independent Palestinian state with provisional borders through a process of Israeli-Palestinian engagement, launched by the international conference. As part of this process, implementation of prior agreements, to enhance maximum territorial contiguity, including further action on settlements in conjunction with establishment of a Palestinian state with provisional borders.

- Enhanced international role in monitoring transition, with the active, sustained, and operational support of the Quartet.

- Quartet members promote international recognition of Palestinian state, including possible UN membership.

Phase III: Permanent Status Agreement and End of the Israeli-Palestinian Conflict — 2004 — 2005

Progress into Phase III, based on consensus judgment of Quartet, and taking into account actions of both parties and Quartet monitoring. Phase III objectives are consolidation of reform and stabilization of Palestinian institutions, sustained, effective Palestinian security performance, and Israeli-Palestinian negotiations aimed at a permanent status agreement in 2005.

- **Second International Conference:** Convened by Quartet, in consultation with the parties, at beginning of 2004 to endorse agreement reached on an independent Palestinian state with provisional borders and formally to launch a process with the active, sustained, and operational support of the Quartet, leading to a final, permanent status resolution in 2005, including on borders, Jerusalem, refugees, settlements; and, to support progress toward a comprehensive Middle East settlement between Israel and Lebanon and Israel and Syria, to be achieved as soon as possible.

- Continued comprehensive, effective progress on the reform agenda laid out by the Task Force in preparation for final status agreement.

- Continued sustained and effective security performance, and sustained, effective security cooperation on the bases laid out in Phase I.

- International efforts to facilitate reform and stabilize Palestinian institutions and the Palestinian economy, in preparation for final status agreement.

- Parties reach final and comprehensive permanent status agreement that ends the Israel-Palestinian conflict in 2005, through a settlement negotiated between the parties based on UNSCR 242, 338, and 1397, that ends the occupation that began in 1967, and includes an agreed, just, fair, and realistic solution to the refugee issue, and a negotiated resolution on the status of Jerusalem that takes into account the political and religious concerns of both sides, and protects the religious interests of Jews, Christians, and Muslims worldwide, and fulfills the vision of two states, Israel and sovereign, independent, democratic and viable Palestine, living side-by-side in peace and security.

- Arab state acceptance of full normal relations with Israel and security for all the states of the region in the context of a comprehensive Arab-Israeli peace.

Appendix B

PETITION TO
DEFEND ISRAEL

Show your commitment to Israel, our friend and ally, by signing the "Petition to Stand in Defense of Israel" today!

Petition to Stand in Defense of Israel
To President George W. Bush;
To Members of the U.S. Senate;
And To Members of the U.S. House of Representatives

Mr. President, as a proud American, I congratulate you for your courageous stand during Operation Iraqi Freedom. Indeed, the people of Iraq have been liberated, and Saddam, and his *Evil Empire* are out of Iraq, and on the run, and our troops, and America, are out of harm's way in Iraq.

However, I am deeply troubled that our ally, Israel, is being forced to pay the appeasement bill with land. The P.L.O. is still a terrorist organization and has sent many Palestinians into Iraq with money and with martyrdom instructions to kill Americans. To force Israel to withdraw its troops from the territories when they are in harm's way is not acceptable. To demand that Palestinian prisoners be released is not acceptable. They burned American flags and celebrated when Americans died in Iraq.

America's war on terrorism began on September 11th. Mayor Rudolph Giuliani was the first U.S. leader to challenge an attempt to create a linkage between Islamic terrorism and Israel. After Saudi Prince Alwaleed stated, "I believe that the United States should re-examine its policies in the Middle East, and adopt a more balanced stance toward the Palestine cause," Giuliani rejected a $10 million check from the Saudi prince, and said that Alwaleed's statements were "highly irresponsible and dangerous." Mr. President, please do not create linkage between America's war against terrorists in Iraq and Israel. If anyone is to be strongly pressured, it should be the P.L.O., not Israel.

To weaken Israel is to create linkage between Baghdad and the Jewish people, and would send a signal to the would-be Osamas and Saddams that there is a justification for terror.

James Baker advised you to "follow your father's 1991 tradition" and "seize the moment." I believe that your beloved father made a serious mistake after the Gulf War in 1991 when he forced Israel to Madrid for a land giveaway. I pray that you will not make the same mistake.

On April 16th, U.S. troops captured Abu Abbas in Baghdad, the mastermind of the terrorist attack on the Achille Lauro when Leon Klinghoffer, a defenseless old man in a wheelchair, was killed and his body and wheelchair thrown overboard. Leon Klinghoffer and his wife, Marilyn, had taken the cruise to celebrate their 36th wedding anniversary. According to the U.S. State Department, Abu Abbas was a member of the Palestine Liberation Organization's executive committee from 1984 to 1991. The U.S. Justice Department has said it has no grounds to seek his extradition, since there are no outstanding warrants against him. Will that same litmus test be applied to the Abu Abbas's in Israeli jails? Will there now be "good terrorists" and "bad terrorists"?

The Palestine Authority demanded the release of Abu Abbas. The PA spokesperson said that the detention of Abbas in Iraq by U.S. forces violated an interim Middle East peace deal: "We demand the United States release Abu Abbas. It has no right to imprison him," said Palestinian cabinet minister Saeb Erekat.

"The Palestinian-Israeli interim agreement signed on September 28, 1995, stated that members of the Palestinian Liberation Organization must not be detained or tried for matters they committed before the Oslo Peace Accord of September 13, 1993," Erekat stated. He added, "This interim agreement was signed on the U.S. side by President Clinton and his Secretary of State, Warren Christopher."

The U.S. demanded that Israel transfer funds belonging to the Palestine Authority, and issue permits to Palestinians seeking work in Israel. A major way Israel has reduced terrorism, since the interim agreement, has been by restricting the access of would-be terrorists, and by not funding them.

Mr. President, we humbly appeal to you not to jeopardize the security and the lives of the Jewish people, and the land of the Bible, for the sake of political expediency. Sir, our young people (troops) are defending our freedom, as are the young people of Israel. We must defend them with our prayers and actions today. Terrorists must not be rewarded.

The so-called "Road Map Plan" calls not only for the recognition of a P.L.O. state, but also for Israel to return all lands not in their possession prior to 1967 to the P.L.O. This includes dividing Jerusalem, and placing virtually all-Christian holy sites in the hands of Islam, putting all Christians in that territory under Islamic rule of law. We strongly oppose this.

The P.L.O. remains a terrorist organization. They continue to support, finance, and promote suicide attacks within the Bible land. They have been responsible for over 2,300 acts of terrorism worldwide. These include the killing of several U.S. diplomats.

Mr. President, to ask Israel to recognize a terrorist organization such as the P.L.O. as a state violates America's "National Strategy for Combating Terrorism." This document has clearly stated National Security objectives such as:

- "To destroy terrorists and their organizations;
- To deny sponsorship, support, and sanctuary to terrorists;
- To end the state sponsorship of terrorism;
- To eliminate terrorist sanctuaries and havens."

The P.L.O. continues to aid, harbor, and support terrorist organizations operating within the Territories. Following a plague of terrorist attacks over the years, the State Department has continuously declared that "Arafat needs to take immediate and effective steps to end attacks, and bring those responsible to justice."

Arafat and the P.L.O. have proven that they will not comply with America's war on terrorism. The P.L.O.-controlled territories have become a haven for more terrorist organizations than any spot on the planet. In direct contrast, the State of Israel has made great sacrifices, and has become a bulwark, readily complying with your terrorism goals and objectives 100 percent.

Mr. President, you have announced that the moment the P.L.O. appoints Mahmoud Abbas as prime minister, and Abbas appoints his cabinet (and he has already said the majority will be Fatah members,) the Road Map will be released, and the process will be fast-tracked. (This will unify the world against Israel—a sovereign State.)

Abbas is not a friend of peace. He was pivotal in the P.L.O.'s rejection of Israel's comprehensive peace plan at Camp David, and has publicly stated he believes the Holocaust was a myth.

He is not a solution to the Palestinian problem, but simply the P.L.O. with a new face. Abbas' cabinet is made up of Fatah hard-liners, most of whom are Arafat's men. Mr. Arafat, the president of the governing Palestine Authority, can fire Mr.Abbas, but he only needs the parliament to form a government. Abbas has con-cluded, however, that without Mr. Arafat's blessings, his cabinet will not get a majority.

You realized that in Afghanistan the Taliban had to be rooted out, not just Osama. You realized the same thing in Iraq. Mr. President, please allow Israel to apply that same standard to the P.L.O. groups designated by the U.S. State Department as "ter--rorist organizations" operating in the P.L.O. territories. These include Hamas, Hizbullah, PLF, PIJ, PFLP (Palestine Front for the Liberation of Palestine), Palestine Islamic Jihad, and the Popular Front for the Liberation of Palestine.

I realize that the United States is under pressure from Russia, the United Nations, the European Union, and the Arab world to sacrifice Israel to appease these countries. I realize that the Quartet is the sponsor of this plan, which you support. The Quartet places no more importance on Israel, than they do on Istanbul, and count Jerusalem no more significant than Johannesburg.

I believe one of the reasons America has been blessed over the years is because we have stood by Israel. I am a Christian who believes the Bible. I am also a proud American who loves my country, and desires the blessings of God to be upon our nation. *"I will bless them that bless thee"* (Genesis 12:3 KJV).

I pray that God will bring revival to America, to the nation of Israel, and revival to the Arab people. However, it cannot come if we compromise moral principles and the biblical values upon which our nation was built. (2 Chronicles 7:14.)

I believe the bond between America and Israel is a moral imperative. I consider that bond to be a biblical mandate. History records that God deals with nations in accordance with how those nations deal with Israel. For biblical reasons first and foremost, I support the State of Israel. "'I will plant them in their land, and no longer shall they be pulled up from the land I have given them,' says the LORD your God" (Amos 9:15). For humanitarian reasons, I support the Jewish people. And for historical reasons, I believe that God gave the land of Israel to the Jewish people.

I am praying that your biblical values and moral conviction will prevail, and that you will strongly oppose the Road Map.

To sign this petition, please go to www.jpteam.org. If you do not have Internet access, write to us at: Jerusalem Prayer Team, P.O. Box 910, Euless, TX 76039. We will send a copy of the petition for you to sign. If you would like more than one copy, please indicate that in your letter. Once we have collected one million signatures, the petition will be presented to the President.

Appendix C

JOIN THE JERUSALEM PRAYER TEAM!

"Pray for the peace of Jerusalem" Psalm 122:6

The Jerusalem Prayer Team is an intercessory movement to "guard, protect, and defend Eretz Yisrael until the Redeemer comes to Zion." This prayer movement was launched in June 2002 by Mike Evans. The Jerusalem Prayer Team established the goal of enlisting one million members to pray daily for the peace of Jerusalem according to Psalm 122:6.

The Jerusalem Prayer Team was birthed out of a one hundred year prayer meeting at the ten Boom home in Holland. It ended when the family was taken to the prison camps for saving 800 Jewish lives. Three hundred prominent American leaders such as Dr. Tim LaHaye, Rev. Joyce Meyer, Dr. Pat Robertson, and Mrs. Anne Graham Lotz, along with thousands around the world are part of this prayer movement.

Name _____

Address _____

City _____ State_____ Zip _____

Email _____

Phone_____

Be a part of prophecy today by joining.
Membership is free.
For more information, please visit our website at www.jpteam.org.

Free gifts for new members.
Jerusalem Prayer Team • P.O. Box 910 • Euless, TX 76039-0910

About the Author

Michael D. Evans is a *Time* magazine best-selling author. He has written seventeen books. His three latest books include: *The Prayer of David: In Times of Trouble*, *The Unanswered Prayers of Jesus*, and *Why Christians Should Support Israel*. All are available in local bookstores, or by contacting his office.

Rev. Evans has appeared on BBC, the *Good Morning Show* in London, *Good Morning America*, *Nightline*, and *Crossfire*. His articles have been published in newspapers throughout the world, including the *Wall Street Journal* and the *Jerusalem Post*.

He has been a confidante to most of Israel's prime ministers, and to both of Jerusalem's mayors. He is the recipient of numerous awards, including the distinguished Ambassador Award by the State of Israel.

Rev. Evans is a dynamic speaker who has spoken at more than 4,000 churches, and in 41 stadiums worldwide. His voice has been heard from the Royal Palace in Madrid to the Kremlin Palace in Moscow. He has been on the cutting-edge of events in Israel for more than two decades...from the state funeral of Yitzhak Rabin to the signing of the Peace Accords in 1993, and the 43rd General Assembly of the United Nations in Geneva.

In addition, Mr. Evans hosts prayer summits in local churches throughout the world with national and international leaders. The Honorable Ehud Olmert, former mayor of Jerusalem, and now Vice Premier of Israel, and former Prime Minister Benjamin Netanyahu, are personal friends of Rev. Evans, and strong supporters of the Jerusalem Prayer Team. Mr. Evans' wife, Carolyn, is the founder of the Christian Woman of the Year Association. This organization has presented awards to such notable women as Ruth Graham, Elizabeth Dole, Mother Teresa, Vonette Bright, Didi Robertson, and Shirley Dobson.

Mike and Carolyn reside in Fort Worth, Texas. They are the parents of four children, Michelle, Shira, Rachel, and Michael David. They have three grandchildren, Jason, Ashley, and Joshua.

Michael D. Evans
Telephone: (817) 268-1228
FAX: (817) 285-0962
E-mail: jpteam@sbcglobal.net

Please include your prayer requests and comments when you contact the author.

Remi Levi, Ambassador to the Americas for the Ministry of Tourism, presents Mike Evans with the Ambassador Award at NRB, February 2003

A Night to Honor Israel, organized by Mike Evans to honor Jerusalem's first Mayor, Teddy Kollek. Standing from left to right: Dr. Mike Evans, Mayor Teddy Kollek, Dr. W. A. Criswell, and Dr. Ben Armstrong

Mike Evans with American soldiers in Beirut

Menachem Begin endorses "Israel: America's Key to Survival" in 1980, Mike Evans' first book

Mike Evans praying
with Prime Minister
Shimon Peres

Mike Evans comforts
terror victims in Israel

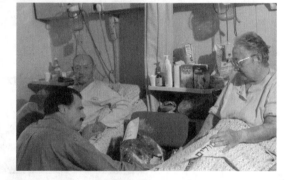

Mike Evans (left) with
American soldiers in
Somalia, October 1993

Jerusalem Mayor Ehud
Olmert and Dr. Mike
Evans at the press con-
ference to launch the
Jerusalem Prayer Team,
June 2002

New York Mayor Rudolph Giuliani and
Mike Evans in New York City, 2003

Mike Evans presents Prime Minister
Yitzhak Shamir with ½ million names of
Christians who have pledged their
prayers and support to Israel

Mike Evans with his dear friend
of 25 years, Finance Minister
Benjamin Netanyahu

Corrie ten Boom clockshop restored
and opened in 1985, Haarlem, Holland

Mike Evans champions Israel at the
Royal Palace in Madrid during the
Middle East Peace Conference

"He who has an ear, let him hear what the Spirit says to the churches. To him who overcomes I will give some of the hidden manna to eat. And I will give him a white stone, and on the stone a new name written which no one knows except him who receives it"' (Revelation 2:17).

Visit our website at:
www.whitestonebooks.com

WHITE STONE BOOKS
LAKELAND, FLORIDA